C-Suite Secrets for Running
Your Career Like a Business

LIKE A
BOSS

*How Top Executives
Elevate Status, Grow Wealth,
& Protect Their Downside*

ELISABETH CONSTANTIN

ISBN: 979-8-9927994-0-8 (Hardcover)
ISBN: 979-8-9927994-1-5 (Paperback)
ISBN: 979-8-9927994-2-2 (eBook)

Library of Congress Control Number: 2025934746
Printed in Brentwood, Tennessee, USA by ABREO Executive Services, LLC

Author photos by Tausha Dickinson. Cover design by Kelly Nielson.

For more information, visit www.theabreofirm.com.

For bulk book orders, contact econstantin@theabreofirm.com

No guts, no glory.
No hustle, no story.

For our corporate and private clients

ABREO has been a trusted partner for senior executives from some
of the world's most high-profile companies.
Serving you through the peaks and valleys of your journey
has been the honor of a lifetime.

Thank you—for everything.

CONTENTS

PART I
FRAMEWORK RESET — TEAR UP THE
CAREER RULEBOOK

Your Career is Not a Charity

PART II
ELEVATING YOUR EXECUTIVE EDGE —
HABITS, KNOWLEDGE, & EXPOSURE 33

Next-Level Gravitas: Diversifying Your Executive Presence

Own Your Brand: The (Seemingly) Little Things

PART III
PEOPLE BUY PEOPLE — YOUR PERSONALITY IS YOUR WINNING EDGE. **163**

Unlock Your Best Self: Developing Your Personality

To protect our clients' and advocates' confidentiality, all names have been changed.

Your Bonus Gifts:
Complimentary Executive Transition Resources from ABREO

Thank you for purchasing *Like A Boss*.

In *Like A Boss*, you'll discover that extraordinary leaders—those who reach the upper echelons of corporate careers—consistently excel in continuous learning, relationship management, and decisive action. In executive transitions, success hinges on diligent preparation and organization.

To help you elevate your path to upper management, I invite you to take advantage of ABREO's proprietary **Executive Transition Checklist & Communication Tracker**. Normally included in every executive service package, I'm pleased to offer them as complimentary gifts exclusively for *Like A Boss* readers.

These resources will guide you through methodical market re-entry preparation and help you track critical conversations with high-profile stakeholders as your network grows with your career—today, tomorrow, and for years to come.

To receive your gifts along with our quarterly publication, *The Executive Club* (unsubscribe at any time), visit:

www.theabreofirm.com/gift and provide your email address. **Page password: LABGift**

I'm rooting for you—you are well on your way. And if you ever need additional support during high-profile market transitions, you know where to find us.

To your success and prosperity,

Elisabeth Constantin
ABREO Executive Services, LLC
Nashville, TN

Preface

"Knowledge is power." —**Sir Francis Bacon**

Some call our work the *hidden* side of the corporate people business—*the dark side*.

While I don't necessarily agree with that label, it does make for a good introduction. As a corporate outplacement provider, my company, ABREO, helps both departing leaders and their organizations move forward gracefully after an involuntary exit—quietly and behind the scenes.

Through our work, we gain insight into many valuable lessons and interesting transition and exit circumstances. The way I like to phrase it is: we support leaders through a time of change, walking alongside them during pivotal moments in their growth—both in business and in life.

I wrote this book for established, new, and future generation leaders like yourself so you can make more out of your executive career and avoid costly mistakes as you ascend to the upper ranks. With a fair dose of realism, *Like A Boss* offers wisdom and insights on how top-level executives maximize their wealth, protect their downside, and expand into high-value territories that elevate their profiles while unlocking opportunities to generate returns far beyond the traditional corporate career path.

During my decade in HR, I couldn't find a body of knowledge that candidly packages this behind-the-scenes information. That's why I wrote this book: so you don't have to learn the secrets of successful top executives the hard way.

The reason this information is so hard to come by is because upper-echelon careers are inherently secretive. The executive world is largely invisible, making it a challenging space to navigate. Ordinary job search journeys don't compare to how executive opportunities are created and realized, how wealth and status are built, or how networks need to be curated and leveraged at the top.

Considering how my own journey began, it's rather ironic that supporting leaders from some of the world's most powerful companies became my life's work. However, once you understand my story, it's probably not all that surprising.

When I arrived in the Midwestern United States shortly after the last recession, I had nothing but a suitcase, my diplomas, and less than five thousand dollars in the bank. That was my life savings after funding my second round of grad school in Germany.

I had no contacts, no network, no mentors, and no sponsors. My unpolished English missed the mark for corporate America, but that hardly mattered since I couldn't even get into the *lobby* of a potential employer. I didn't know how to write a resume for the American market, and I was clueless about what's commonly referred to as the 'black hole of recruiting.' A rookie fresh from the boat, I didn't know anything, and I spoke funny. Not the best starting position, but here I was off to the races.

My low point came when I stopped counting the number of rejections. It must have been sometime after I had diligently prepared and submitted over three hundred job applications without getting a single interview call. This was five months into my job search. Expecting to find my footing soon, given my transferable qualifications and experience, I had recently splurged a thousand dollars on a used car. The money was running out, and I started to fear I was going to be cooked.

I will never forget a summer day in 2012. Stressed about the entire situation, I put ten dollars worth of gas into the tank and drove into the city. I had no particular destination in mind; I just needed to get out, so I headed to the business district. The afternoon sun sparkled across the mirrored facades of the high-rises and office buildings around me. The professional lunch crowd was leaving the local restaurants—smartly dressed people with big smiles and bigger paychecks. They lived the nine-to-five dream I was chasing so desperately but couldn't seem to catch.

As I was driving around, the phone rang. It was my family calling from home, asking how things were going. *Again.* I pulled over and gave them my most convincing *"Any day now, really!"* response. Being protective and concerned, they cautiously asked if I had considered coming home.

Something inside me broke. After we hung up, it all came out—my worries about finding corporate work, and even more so, the realization that I was out of my depth and out of place. My American dream had just received the reality check of a lifetime.

The proof was right there: tears running down my face as I considered my current circumstances. Parked by the curb in my beaten-up Chrysler in Clayton, one of St. Louis' nicer areas, I closed my eyes and leaned my forehead against the steering wheel, ashamed.

"You don't have what it takes. You don't belong here," whispered the voice inside my head. Since people were looking, it had to be true. Here I was, unable to even afford lunch. The bitter reality was that, after 300+ applications, I still had no results. My family was right. If I didn't want to flip burgers with two advanced degrees—something I seriously began to consider— maybe I should think about going home.

The short version: It was a close call, but eventually, I made it—furiously kicking at the proverbial darkness until it revealed a glimmer of light. In the end, it was perfecting the art of financials-based resume writing that saved me, paving the way for an executive-centric HR career and, a decade later, the launch of ABREO.

When the universe finally caved, it sent me *one* single phone call. Not particularly generous, if you ask me, but in the end, that's all it took: one call, one conversation, one person who gave me an opportunity that helped me build from there. Since this book isn't about me, the rest of the story is tucked away in the back if you're curious about how it all went down.

To whoever came up with the saying that the job search is a numbers game, *chapeau!* Hearing that phrase really used to piss me off, even though today I say it to *my* clients all the time. Given how long job searches take at the top level, it typically annoys them too. *Full circle, I guess.*

Today, I am one of the most trusted resume writers in the North American executive market. World-class leaders from companies like Goldman Sachs, Microsoft, and Porsche choose to work with ABREO and refer us to others. Word has spread that we are among the best in the industry at assertively positioning leaders' accomplishments and financial metrics for promotions and stealth searches.

Eventually, ABREO caught the attention of Chief Legal Officers and Chief Human Resources Officers from major corporations. They now engage my company to give their departing executives a better leg up after involuntary terminations—a service also known as 'outplacement support.'

Life surely works in mysterious ways. Twelve years ago, I couldn't even land an entry-level job in corporate America. Today, Fortune 500 companies bring me in to guide their departing leaders through the executive search process in the invisible job market—all the way up to the C-suite.

If that's not leveling up, then I don't know what is. Since leveling up is essentially the DNA and message of this book, let's grow together.

Like A Boss.

INTRODUCTION:

This Book Will Challenge You!

*"Honesty is the first chapter in the book
of wisdom."*
—Thomas Jefferson

According to Gallup roughly two-thirds of employees seem to largely view corporate environments as a place where the spirit goes to die.[1]

Corporate careers can be incredibly rewarding—in so many ways. They can also be incredibly tough. For most people, the truth lies somewhere in the middle. Essentially, executives hire us to learn some truths they don't always get to hear—about themselves, corporations, and careers in general.

In the world of work and corporate messaging, real honesty is a rare commodity. With this sentiment and Gallup's engagement numbers in mind, it's no surprise that industry executives have been asking for this book, saying: *"People need to know the full picture of all the levers they can pull to maximize their career and protect their downside, so they don't have to learn incrementally or by mistake."*

Why am I the one writing this book?

ABREO originally started as a pure document business. In the beginning, I focused solely on delivering financials-based resumes to help upper management clients secure introductions and conversations at the highest levels, fostering new opportunities.

My customers, seasoned executives from director-level to C-suite, soon sought additional support. They began to request a more robust body of knowledge to navigate and self-advocate during the executive search process, make more money, secure their downside, and incorporate opportunities into their long-term career planning that wouldn't just enhance and fast-track their overall trajectory, but also serve as a corporate exit strategy with additional future revenue streams.

Based on ABREO's client education curriculum and my experience working with senior leaders for over a decade across HR and outplacement, *Like A Boss* offers this body of knowledge. It will also challenge the way you think about pursuing your executive career—at least if you want to avoid the kinds of mistakes that often cost people dearly.

The first time I seriously considered writing this book was when Lucas, a seasoned and progressive Chief Human Resources Officer, told me, *"You should do it, especially now that you're no longer in the corporate world. HR can't talk about it, and individual C-level leaders won't, because nobody wants to give up their competitive edge!"*

Lucas had trusted ABREO to help a high-profile leader from his organization get back into the market after things didn't work out. Our relationship grew quite close during that collaboration. In one of our conversations, he shared something personal with me: *"Elisabeth, had I known some of the information you give your clients earlier in my career, I wouldn't have had to grow as old as an elephant to gain this wisdom. I could have saved time, energy, and made a lot more money. Even many of my colleagues—seasoned CHROs who should know better from everything they see behind the scenes—are widely naive about safeguarding their own downsides."*

Wow, I thought. *If even HR leaders with 20+ years of experience handling business and terminations struggle with this, how does everyone else stand a chance?*

You probably purchased this book looking for an inspiring career development read. Maybe you are in middle management planning for upward mobility. Maybe you are a credentialed executive with a 'there's always more to learn' mindset. Or maybe you simply want to sail through work with a bit more gravitas, refinement, knowledge, levity, and money so you won't find yourself surprised by the rainy days that are an inevitable part of every career. Good for you!

Let's begin with what *Like A Boss* is not.

This is not a traditional book on leadership development focused on the art of influencing and leading others. You should absolutely continue growing those skills and leverage appropriate resources. Here's another thing *Like A Boss* doesn't do: it doesn't cover the basics. Obviously, you need to be excellent at your job, secure mentors and sponsors, apply yourself, keep learning, stay humble, and add value beyond simply doing the basics of your role. Talent is worthless without execution; you can't be an empty suit. Even though one might wonder how some people get ahead, when push comes to shove, mediocrity usually doesn't make it to the top—at least not for long.

Like A Boss is a street-smarts book.

Like A Boss is about how to lead yourself and upgrade your knowledge in behaviors and strategies that upper management individuals typically use to increase gravitas, expand financially, and protect their downside. In the end, it all boils down to one thing: more money, power, and status—or at least maintaining it—and reducing risk to your assets. Let's keep it real: with the exception of those who've already made their money in life, very few people go to work just for fun. For most of us, mortgages, student loans, or ex-spouse alimony need to be paid.

In doing my research, I asked executives what they would want out of this book. The answer, repeatedly, was: *"I realize I might need to change how I think about my career and expand. Teach me how top-level executives play and scale their game so I can get a leg up. With a book that's practical, for real-world application, brief and digestible, and—most importantly—honest."* Not a small order.

As a practitioner's guide from and for executives, *Like A Boss* incorporates literally centuries of practical, real-world experience and behind-the-scenes knowledge from global C-level executives who have served in multi-billion-dollar companies of our present lifetime. It also includes insights from anonymous voices—CHROs, Chief Legal Officers, and executive headhunters—who, like Lucas, believe that gaining more wisdom earlier is critical for success and raises the tide for all boats.

Because true authenticity is rare these days, I decided to incorporate anonymized real-life stories and lessons directly in leaders' voices, whenever possible. Executives, no matter how high their star may shine, are people first. As a result, the examples range from humorous to cutthroat, with some resembling Shakespearean tragedies.

No matter where you are in your career, you've already demonstrated many high-achiever qualities to have come this far in your professional journey. Intellectual and social curiosity, work ethic, integrity, discipline, political savvy, collaboration, relationship-building, emotional intelligence, and the ability to accept feedback—all these talents you've accumulated. Congratulations, you're well on your way and have achieved so much already. I applaud your belief that you are worthy of more, *because you are.*

I'm frequently invited to deliver motivational and informational speeches on executive career ROI at industry conferences, Ivy League executive clubs, and workshops with companies like Dell Technologies. In these settings, I help leaders uncover the additional tools they can use to maximize their wins.

There are always two types of audience reactions: With the optimists in the room, the lightbulbs go on, and they get excited about new ways to build their paths to greater success and status. The pessimists, on the other hand, immediately shut down, thinking, *I don't even want to consider how much potential and money I've left on the table, and I'm not ready to change.* Clearly, you're an optimist with a builder's mindset, or you wouldn't have bought this book. Congratulations!

Initially, my first title choice for this book was *Kingship*, because that's what we all have in common. Every day, we set out to build our personal worlds and professional kingdoms. In the end, I chose *Like A Boss* because I didn't want to put the cart before the horse.

Building a kingdom is, first and foremost, a matter of wisdom, knowledge, mindset, and a 'doing-more' attitude. That's why the cover features an elephant. They symbolize wisdom, good fortune, power, and positivity. If you look closely, you'll notice the elephant also incorporates a crown—representing the empire you're building.

On behalf of every seasoned executive who contributed to *Like A Boss*, I wish you three things for your career:

- ▶ **Successes *and* teachable moments alike, for they will help you evolve.**
- ▶ **The foresight to always protect your downside.**
- ▶ **To never lose sight of what matters most: *you, your family, and paying it forward to lift others up.***

Let's get your educational journey started by challenging your thinking and learning from the best. As the saying by Mohit Manke goes: *"First LEARN. Then remove the L."*

PART I

Framework Reset
Tear Up the Career Rulebook

Your Career is Not a Charity

The most accomplished senior executives I had the privilege of serving are best described as corporate realists. They embody a deep understanding and acceptance of the often-contradictory nature of human behavior, the bottom-line focus of businesses, and what this constant balancing act means for their success.

In the first section of *Like A Boss*, we will get real about the cut-throat realities of how everyone around you thinks, the way for-profit corporations must operate, and why the idea of treating your career more like a business might be a north star pathway that can yield significantly higher returns than running a charity operation.

Challenging some outdated career thinking is a great way to begin evolving how you view work and life.

Let's get real.

CHAPTER 1

How Your Competitors Think—
The Playbook You're Up Against

"There is no friendship in trade."
—Benjamin Franklin

Here is an anecdote about protecting competitive advantage from a conversation I once overheard at Harvard, just to drive home what you're up against:

John, a Business Unit Leader in a large company, is telling Anna how he recently got a big bonus for his double-digit P&L growth. John is using the reward to build another extension to his already impressive home. Coincidentally, another BU Leader from the same company, Henry, lives in John's neighborhood. They are friendly. Anna asks John, *"So, since you're both in the same company and are friends, are you going to tell Henry how you did it?"* John almost spits into his drink, finding the idea to give away his competitive advantage completely absurd. John likes Henry, *but not that much.*

John simply responds with a long drawn out *"Naaaah"* and a knowing smile as he knocks back his Old Fashioned, chuckling at Anna's naiveté.

Here's what most people in John's position think: *I may play golf with Henry and we have him and Sandy over for dinner a couple times a year, mostly to brag about our new vacation home and the cost of private school in Switzerland for the twins, but screw that guy! He doesn't need to know how I pulled this off. Plus, I don't care about the company—I'm already planting seeds in the industry on who is behind the growing market share and rising stock price. Recruiters will start calling after the next earnings call and I'm off to the races for more money. So, screw Henry and everyone else and cheerio.*

If you're laughing, it's because you know it's true. John isn't going to give Henry the secret sauce that just gave him more power in the company, sets him up for new outside opportunities, *and* made him the winner of the neighborhood's square footage ego showdown. *Absolutely not!*

John is holding the crown at a high-point of life. The king will always do whatever it takes to stay at the top for as long as possible. *Why?* Because wise kings *know* their success won't last forever! The tide could change. The pendulum of life will swing the other way.

What's happening here? This real-life situation is a prime example of survival instincts at work. Our brains are wired around scarcity. Everyone looks out for themselves first—a harsh reality of human behavior that can be tough for more idealistic individuals to accept.

If you have the expectation that in our advanced evolutionary state we should be better than our primitive survival-based brain wiring, you're not entirely unreasonable. *I hear you.* But given how long it has taken the human race to get this far, you could be waiting for a while. Even Napoleon once said, *"Men are moved by two levers only: fear and self-interest."* Napoleon died two hundred years ago. Rapid progress doesn't seem to be on the horizon here.

Because of what ABREO does—helping executives privately with their transitions or getting them back on track when their employer brings us in during a termination—I'm often asked what it *really* takes to get ahead and stay there; the next level, the C-suite summit, on corporate boards, or to financial independence.

Most people intuitively suspect that achieving top-level careers and financial freedom requires more than just hard work and playing nice in the sandbox. They're right. The devil, however, is always in the details. While no one stays at the top forever, the formula for climbing up typically boils down to the three foundational P's: Performance, Personality, and Politics—along with knowing more and doing *more*; all with a positive attitude. It sounds simple, but for most of us, it's a lifetime of learning. Ultimately, it starts with the right mindset to evolve and the foresight to prepare for inevitable rainy days.

You've probably read the quote at the beginning of this book: 'No guts, no glory. No hustle, no story.' Commonly attributed to the U.S. military, these words resonate with many senior leaders. More importantly, it's the implication behind these eight words that matters: through effort and risk-taking, even though we can't always predict or control the outcomes, we are still in charge of much of our destiny. This mindset directly translates to the need for personal responsibility in shaping your own path as you ascend to the summit.

Here's what I mean by that. Great careers don't *just happen* to people. Successful businesses don't *just happen*. Being an incredible cook, singer, or what have you, doesn't *just happen*. While it's true that in corporate power dynamics others will always, to a certain extent, have a say over whether we will get hired, promoted, cut loose, etc., we are more in charge than we often want to believe.

Highly successful leaders fundamentally understand that they are in the driver's seat when it comes to building their empires. They relentlessly embrace and execute two of life's core philosophical and physical concepts:

1. **Panta Rei** (Greek for 'everything flows,' meaning that everything is in constant motion, up and down, and nothing ever stays the same): Just like life is full of peaks and valleys, so too are careers. John understands that the tide can shift quickly, which is why he works hard to protect his position. The takeaway here is that valleys—like losing a job, getting passed over for a promotion, or experiencing a demotion—are a part of life's cyclical nature. They should be expected, not feared. So, prepare for them. Bring that umbrella and strap on that golden parachute. When you're flying at ten thousand feet all the time, you're going to need it sooner or later. While a few people *seem* to get lucky and dodge all the bullets, thinking that smooth sailing is always the norm is not realistic. Also, if you haven't noticed, with people who 'get lucky' in their careers, there is a high chance they are fighting their battles elsewhere in life like with their health, relationships, or in other areas.

2. **Momentum:** When we put ourselves in motion—without waiting for perfection—by learning, applying ourselves, building relationships, taking risks, and intentionally stepping into uncomfortable situations while daring to

think differently, we begin setting things in motion. This isn't abstract theory, but rather what in physics is known as momentum and chain reactions. Regardless of the ups, downs, rainy days, and curveballs, energy and effort create momentum, momentum creates opportunities, and opportunities build kingdoms.

In other words, senior executives get where they are not only through skill, competence, and savviness, but by *courageously doing more* (and with a magnetic personality). Mahatma Gandhi said, *"Where you will be in five years depends on what you do today."* I love this quote, as it reinforces the fact that all of us can achieve so much more if we simply move from thinking to doing.

When I speak about this, there's always one person in the audience who pushes back, arguing that while executives are people like you and me, not everyone can make it to the top.

It's true. Not everyone will be king. Mainly for three reasons:

1. Not everyone is willing to do what it takes (learn more and do more). Not everyone brings the relentless discipline, grit, or frankly, the desire to make the required sacrifices to inch-crawl to the summit. That's fine. That's actually good news, because those people are automatically not your competition.

2. Some people, despite being very intelligent, simply don't have even a somewhat advanced level of political savviness and the kind of endearing personality that makes it easy for them to build the necessary alliances and relationships. They are also not your competition.

3. Despite best-in-class skills, effort, execution, savviness, and personality, some very qualified people just won't make it. That too is part of life.

Staying stagnant is a choice. Effort still gets most people a lot further than those who don't try as hard, or at all. Remember how careers—like life—are an up and down? You win some, you lose some. If you like a sports analogy, Roger Federer once nailed it in his Dartmouth commencement speech when he explained that nobody wins every point and every game. [2] The rewards of choosing to play, improving our game by outworking your opponents, and winning *sometimes* will still get most people further than doing nothing, irrespective of whether you make it *all* the way to the top or merely come close. Getting close is still *pretty damn good.*

Here is the bottom line: Growth is optional, but unless something structurally changes and everyone suddenly overrides their survival-based brain programming that enabled our species to survive for the past millions of years, you'll be up against people like John who skillfully and savagely look out for themselves first. You can fight it with moral righteousness, or you can accept *what is* and play their game. It's the way the world works. No one says you have to like it.

Whether you reach John's level or higher—and manage to stay there for a while—will largely depend on your willingness to learn more, do more, and safeguard yourself for the rainy days. Picking up a few more tricks of the trade and applying them will make your corporate ascent easier, faster, and more profitable.

In addition to understanding and accepting human nature and how people operate, it's crucial to understand how businesses think. Hint: businesses are made up of people.

Let's unpack this.

Boss-Minded Leaders Challenge the Status Quo by Asking Themselves:

▶ What amazing achievements have I already accomplished? (e.g. my degree(s), promotions, awards, industry recognition, current status and gravitas, etc.)

▶ Am I ready to challenge my thinking, learn more, and then take action to do more?

▶ Am I fundamentally understanding and at peace with the fact that there will be peaks and valleys in my path?

CHAPTER 2

How Businesses Think—And What That Means for You

"Corporations have neither bodies to be punished, nor souls to be condemned; they therefore do as they like."
—Edward Thurlow

During my corporate days, I once asked Jenna, a Group CEO in my company back then, if she loved working for us because, unlike her whiny peers, she never complained. We had a great relationship, so she opened up over a cup of coffee one day.

"Listen," she said, *"I probably wouldn't say this on a recorded line, but I guess I like it enough. My expectations are low though. I don't work here because I love this company; it's not my company. But overall, it works for now."* I asked what she meant by that.

"I have autonomy and good challenges, the money is competitive, and I respect the people I work with," she explained. *"There's more to life than this place though, I just don't let anyone know that I feel that way. At the*

end of the day, the mix of money, people, and challenges needs to be worth it. If that ever changes, I'm out. Just like I know that if I don't deliver, they'll cut me loose in a heartbeat. I've been around long enough to know I'm neither special nor irreplaceable."

What a sad, cynical way to think about your work, you might think. *She should just resign and make room for someone who is a little more appreciative and actually wants to work there.* Didn't you say you wanted an honest book about people and careers?

Conversations like these are what I call the 'corporate reality check.' It's the kind of honesty you won't find in HR engagement surveys because, hopefully, everyone knows they aren't truly confidential. Jenna, like John, is what I refer to as a corporate realist. She thinks about herself first and keeps her expectations grounded. Contrary to what you might initially think, Jenna isn't disengaged. In fact, she is highly successful in real life for several reasons.

Psychologically, she knows how to separate her personal life from work. She isn't overly emotionally attached to the company or its people, and she always assesses whether getting up in the morning still makes sense for her. In short, Jenna treats her career like a business. From my experience, leaders like Jenna typically handle involuntary transitions much better than those who over-identify with their work, job, company, or colleagues.

People have a lot of expectations of organizations and work these days. Many believe that, in addition to providing a paycheck, a job should be fun, offer a greater sense of purpose, and foster a family-like sense of belonging. That's all very nice, but given the often-challenging realities of corporate life, it's surprising that people continue to cling to these expectations. At the end of the day, there are two fundamental truths in business:

1. **Organizations exist to add value for their customers and shareholders, make money, and be profitable. Period.** Even charities must generate revenue, or they close their doors. While we understand this on an intellectual level, the potential consequences of this business reality are often something we'd rather ignore.

2. **All organizations are self-serving, just like people. Always.** No matter how altruistic people or companies may want you to believe they are, at the end of the day, everyone does what's best for themselves—including you. Our brains are evolutionarily wired for scarcity and survival, which means *"Me and myself first, at all times."* You are no different, if you're being honest with yourself. Neither are your boss and colleagues. *Facts.*

We live in a time where clear messaging isn't always appreciated. Jenna is way too smart to say what she thinks openly, even though many people feel this way too. It's a huge paradox in western capitalist societies: everyone constantly feels pressure to say how much they *love* their job or *love working* because it's the cultural narrative everyone buys into, or plays along with at least.

Meanwhile employee disengagement numbers show how people *really* think about work. According to Gallup, only 33 percent of US employees were engaged in 2023. This study cites detachment and dissatisfaction from their organization and the fact that nobody cares about them as a person as reasons for lack of engagement. Like Jenna alluded, corporations don't care about employees in the same way a *real* family would. They do whatever they want and need to do. In return, and maybe as a response, two-thirds of employees in this country don't give a hoot about their employer and their jobs (at least not until they lose it), costing the US economy a whopping $1.9 trillion in lost productivity per year.[3] Cause and effect, you might say.

An alternative, more authentic approach would be if leadership could simply acknowledge:

"Our primary goal is to create value for our customers and shareholders, make money, and remain profitable. Our senior executives have two key responsibilities. First, they must lead the organization toward the future, guided by our best forecasting efforts. Second, they must foster a respectful environment where people want to work, not one where

they'd rather stab their eyes out with a fork. The employees we choose to retain are those who don't just deliver great core work, but also add additional value. We want people who conduct themselves in a way that makes collaboration enjoyable when things are easy, and can maintain respect when we have to disagree on the best path to our goals."

I mean, wouldn't it be nice if someone *actually* came out and said that?

The two-thirds Gallup majority who is mentally checked out and exasperated from the common *"We're all one big happy family here at Fun Times Corporation"* ra-ra-rhetoric would probably breathe a sigh of relief and say, *"Well, at least they're being honest."*

It would remove the hypercriticism from what everyone already knows—that everyone is replaceable and periodically someone gets the boot.

At the end of the day, whether the truth everyone knows is spoken out loud or not is irrelevant for your intents and purposes. *This* is what everyone knows and thinks, including your senior leadership teams and upper management: *"Don't expect us to keep you around unless you continue to deliver."* Or Jenna, *"This job is a means to an end."* Or John, *"Me first, always."*

So, what does that mean for you? Be as enthusiastic as you like about work. If you're one of those people who sincerely just *loves* getting up in the morning to go to work, *fantastic*! According to Gallup, the world *clearly* needs more people with your sort of enthusiasm. Just don't lose sight of the fact that you too will be just a number the minute you stop delivering or business conditions change. If you're not enthusiastic about work, that's okay too. You can just pretend and float along which will admittedly be better for your career, at least until something changes about how society generally thinks and talks about work. Like Jenna, you can still be extremely successful.

Whether you love your job or see it as a means to an end, if you can accept the fact that you're fungible, you'll be ahead of most in your journey toward emotional and adult responsibility. Most people stay in a perpetual state of denial about their long-term relevance, placing their emotional stability in the hands of a corporation or their boss' validation and approval. This is a dangerous gamble with both your psychological and financial health.

Understanding that businesses often make tough decisions where your personal well-being isn't the top priority can catch people off guard. I get it—being part of the collateral damage can be quite the inconvenience.

That's why it's crucial to understand that job security doesn't exist as long as you work for someone else. Once people realize they're 100% replaceable and can't rely on a company to take care of them, they also realize they are 100% responsible for themselves.

Taking full responsibility for yourself and your career requires adopting a new, boss-level way of thinking—similar to how John and Jenna operate. Both treat their careers like businesses that must turn a constant profit. It's a cutthroat departure from previous generations' beliefs, where 'hard work will always be rewarded' was at the forefront of everyone's hopes and thinking.

How do you make that shift? By realizing that running your livelihood like a business requires doing more and advocating for yourself. If you're not mentally prepared to advocate for yourself, you might as well run a charity. Charity is great, but it doesn't pay the bills or build an early retirement nest egg. So, unless you want to work forever, you might have some inner work to do to shift your vintage career thinking.

Let's take a moment to look at some sobering realities of life; that might help.

Boss-Minded Leaders Challenge the Status Quo by Asking Themselves:

▶ Do I truly understand that, as long as I work for someone else, I will always be replaceable?

▶ Can I recognize the benefits of adopting a more realistic perspective on careers? How would this shift affect my stress levels?

▶ What successful leaders do I know who embody the 'corporate realist' mindset? What can I learn from their approach?

CHAPTER 3

P&L Mindset—Run Your Career Like a Business

"To be is to do."
—Immanuel Kant

I was once involved in the offer negotiation process for a BU Leader role. As typical for senior executive compensation, even the slightest change behind the comma would have had significant financial ripple effects for years down the line.

In the 5th round on bonus structures and perks, both sides were beginning to get a little fatigued. When the involved HR Director threw out the latest counteroffer, there was a long pause on the call. Eventually Theo, the candidate, said, *"Look, I get it, but your compensation structures just don't work for me. I run my career like I will run your P&L: like a business, not a charity. I also have a family to support. So, I guess it would help if you guys could get a little creative with the numbers over there or maybe find someone else who needs this job more than I do. I didn't call you; you called me."*

Solid. *Risky approach though.* After the call ended, everyone at the table looked around a little uncomfortably, then someone simply said, *"I respect that."* While they couldn't make things work in the end, I will always remember this conversation as a bold example of no-nonsense candidate self-advocacy.

Like Jenna, John, and Theo, millions of executives around the world understand that selling their time needs to be worthwhile. Top-level careers require significant personal sacrifices. Time is money, but unlike money, none of us can make more time.

Here's a sobering piece of reality, just as a reminder: I, you, and everyone around you will die one day. None of us know when, but *it's going to happen. For real!* Now, here's another provocative question: did you come into this world just to work? How long do you want to work? Going back to those Gallup engagement numbers, it seems that two-thirds of the population would rather not work—at least not for someone else or within corporate ecosystems. Wouldn't it be smarter to find ways to make your money sooner, so you can do whatever you want with your time?

A middle-market CEO I know once said to me: *"The best place in life is when you have the kind of 'stupid money' where you know it will never run out. At that point, nobody can make you do anything you don't want to, but if you decide to play along it won't bother you that much. At that point you realize that at the end of the day none of the drama*

or petty trench wars around you matters. That's true free-
dom, and that's when work can turn into fun."

Once you understand that as long as you choose to work
for someone else, you'll always be a replaceable commodity, the dynamic changes. Treating your career like
a business becomes a logical concept—one you'll know
you need to play lock, stock, and barrel. *Games are fun.*

Playing the self-advocacy game matters because nobody
is coming to save you, nobody will do it for you, and
life is short. Tomorrow isn't guaranteed for anyone, so
being a boss and taking charge will likely yield higher
returns than waiting for things to change or opportunities to *come to you.* Your career's P&L is your responsibility. How profitable it is, is largely up to you.

So why is putting movement and momentum into
campaigning for ourselves so difficult? I blame it on
ingrained beliefs. Our larger socio-economic ecosystem
has an established set of beliefs that we tend to buy into
and accept as truths, whether they serve us or not. In
itself, that's not a bad thing. Shared belief systems help
keep things on track and people and societies in line.
It's like traffic rules—they keep us safe, which is good.
Although, occasionally, I'd argue that a speeding ticket
might be worth it if it gets us to our destination faster.

In the context of work, traditional 'rules' and beliefs
around careers are like a cozy comfort blanket. It may
feel good to hide under that blanket, even when we
know it won't keep us warm in frosty conditions.

Hiding tends to provide a false sense of stability. In the corporate career context, stability is treacherous territory.

Ignoring reality also won't drive the motivation to become your own champion, get you on your way to achieving earlier financial independence and having options. The choice to accept a job (or not), to stay or to go. Without choices, it becomes difficult to say: *"Fun Times Corporation is for the birds. I'm out! Adios...."*

In the next chapter, we'll challenge some long-held, self-limiting career beliefs that have persisted in the collective think tank for far too long. Since you're here for honesty and growth, you'll also receive alternative perspectives that align better with today's work reality—and your long-term goals of financial security and personal freedom.

Let's poke.

Boss-Minded Leaders Challenge the Status Quo by Asking Themselves:

▶ Do I hold any outdated beliefs about careers that I know, deep down, don't serve me?

▶ Have these beliefs hurt me or held me back in my career?

▶ Why have I been holding onto these beliefs? Was that wise?

CHAPTER 4

From Legacy Thinking to New Perspectives

"Convictions are more dangerous foes of truth than lies."
—**Friedrich Nietzsche**

Would you like to solidify and expand your dominance like John? Become more of a detached realist like Jenna? Or feel empowered to campaign for yourself like Theo?

Here are five new realities to burst your legacy thinking bubble and help you operate more like our bold and brave protagonists.

1. Loyalty Pays Off

Old thinking: "Loyalty will be rewarded, I just have to wait long enough."

Rarely. Most people will say that loyalty is pretty dead these days. As a retired HR colleague of mine always used to put it, *"All of us are only as valuable as the job we did yesterday."* Meaning, regardless of past credit, everyone has to re-prove their relevance to our organizations, leaders, peers, and teams *every single day.* Performance review day is coming. Companies will be loyal to you as long as you are useful, but we are all on borrowed time. Even CEOs get fired and directors get removed from boards.

Boss thinking: "I understand loyalty works both ways and is never guaranteed. While I know that I'm replaceable at a moment's notice just like anyone else, I will do my best to learn and expand both personally and professionally and do right by the company while I decide to work here. Yet, the same way a corporation won't hesitate to replace me, I also won't hesitate to move on to a better opportunity should that option present itself. I understand I need to put myself first."

2. Hard Work Pays Off

Old thinking: "Hard work will be rewarded."

It's another one of those core beliefs people want to hold on to. And why not? There is a massive socio-economic upside when everyone buys into that narrative. Employees will work overtime without pay or questioning the expectation. It's also easy to pass blame to those who don't 'win' in the rat race because it's convenient to say, *"I guess so-and-so isn't successful because he or she doesn't try that hard...."* Voilá, everyone can feel better about themselves. And who doesn't like that? As mentioned previously, there are no top-level careers without hard work, but it will be by no means the only factor for your success.

Boss thinking: "I understand that hard work is only one aspect that contributes to my success. I also understand that the higher I go, the more my overall attitude and personality will determine my destiny so I will actively invest not just in optimizing my knowledge and skills, but in developing my personality and relationships as well."

3. Politics Doesn't Matter

Old Thinking: "I can achieve everything on my own."

It's hard to argue with the fundamentals of quantum physics—specifically, the principle of entanglement, which asserts that everything is connected. As human beings within the broader web of socio-economic contexts, we cannot exist or achieve anything in isolation. This is especially true in corporations. Getting things done depends not only on your skill level but also on how well you build relationships, secure buy-in, access resources, and influence others to deliver the work.

Politics and power plays will always exist, with or without you. Over the course of my career, I've met only a handful of people who managed to carve out top-level careers with a neutral, Switzerland-like approach. Their personalities were so favorable that their reputation for doing what was right for their organizations carried them through. That is extremely rare.

A slightly larger, yet still small, group of people manage to glide through corporate life with what seems like no agenda—though, in reality, they are highly political. They play politics, but they disguise it so well, masked by impeccable personalities, that nobody notices. People in these two categories are politically savvy to the point of seeming almost superhuman. That's why they're so rare in corporate ecosystems; they're typically found in the public sector.

For ordinary mortals, strategically aligning with sponsors and influential people while maintaining a broad and healthy relationship web is a socio-economic necessity. This way, they can pivot quickly when circumstances change and the need to reattach to a new leader arises. With the right mindset, politics can also be fun.

Boss thinking: "I understand that in order to elevate myself and gain more visibility and opportunities within my organization and beyond, I need to put in the effort to build relationships with the right people. It's *what* I know, and also *who* I know. I understand that my personality will be a big factor for my success in this area long term and that politics will be played with or without me."

4. Confusing Business and Personal

Old Thinking: "The people in my company are like family."

This is a hard 'hell no.' Given that we spend more time at work than at home, it's understandable why people get attached to their teams and elevate them to family status. But it's unwise. Setting healthy boundaries is a better approach. You are replaceable at a moment's notice. Nobody will dwell on you or your legacy—at least not for long. Public memory is short-lived. In our survival-driven world, others will feel relieved it was you and not them, and quickly move on.

Boss thinking: "While I enjoy the people I work with, I know that teams and situations can change quickly. They could leave, or I could leave, and that's part of business. I will do my best to build relationships, hoping that some will stand the test of time, but I will always remember that work groups are temporary and it's not in my best interests to place my emotional stability and well-being on a corporation and its people. I will reserve that for my friends and family."

5. Human Resources is for the Employee

Old Thinking: "HR is there for me and will support me if something happens."

Sometimes. It makes sense why many people see it that way. Broadcasting 'our people are our most important assets,' showcasing people-centric cultures, and highlighting the numerous great, honorable, and valuable things HR does all contribute to this understanding. HR is always in a tough spot. Hired to serve both the people *and* the company's interests, it can never win the old high school popularity contest.

Some of the finest people I know are in HR, doing great work that serves the people. They recruit talent into organizations, provide opportunities to make a living and contribute to society, enable training and learning, support ongoing career development, and run the numbers on the back end to ensure compensation and benefits remain competitive *(just maybe not too competitive)*.

But just like for most people there are ways *into* organizations, there are also ways *out* of the company, and they are not always the employee's choice. Somebody has to do that job too, and that is also part of HR's responsibility.

I've never met an HR person who enjoyed letting people go. Whether for economic, performance, personality, or even more Machiavellian reasons, most HR professionals have their heart in the right place. But when push comes to shove, their primary purpose is to serve the company's interests first. I'm not saying there's anything wrong with that—it's simply a business reality to understand, accept, and never forget.

Boss thinking: "I always want to remember that HR's first responsibility is to represent the interests of the business. I understand that no matter how good my relationships may be, things can change. People who I respect or like won't hesitate to end my career if they are instructed to do so. Knowing that dynamic, I will be mindful about what information I share, with whom, and when."

Since you've internalized that most corporations and individuals around you operate in ways that benefit themselves first, it's easy to see why increasing your responsibility for career ROI is crucial for your future as a senior leader. *You simply can't afford not to.*

By starting to override your brain's legacy system with new thinking and leveling up your personal accountability for yourself, you're preparing to expand your knowledge, skills, and habits in critical areas of the executive ROI lever portfolio.

While some concepts in this book will be new—especially for younger leaders—seasoned executives will also gain new insights if there are gaps in their self-advocacy history. Other ideas are so fundamental they might surprise you at first. Yet throughout the years, many powerful executives have repeatedly credited consistency in the seemingly simple behaviors as key to their growth and success.

How?

By learning (and then doing) more, *one step at a time.*

Boss-Minded Leaders Challenge the Status Quo by Asking Themselves:

▶ Which of these legacy thinking patterns apply to me, and where should I consider adopting a new mindset?

▶ Which executives in my network model these ways of thinking? What additional lessons can I learn from them?

PART II

Elevating Your Executive Edge
Habits, Knowledge, & Exposure

Boss Basics on Having Your Act Together

While what you will read on the following pages may initially seem basic, the key message here is: have your house in order. For many people, this is more difficult than it looks. The beauty of our life's often messy and complicated reality is that it's usually a work in progress—at least for people with a growth mindset. However, taking responsibility for certain fundamentals is crucial if you want to unleash top performance.

That's not to say every executive lives a perfect life (far from it, actually). But leaders who make it to the summit tend to strive for a certain level of stability and discipline in key areas of life: health, cultivating quality relationships and interests, financial discipline, and time management.

A common pushback we hear is: *"I don't have time for all this; I'm too busy."* Really? How much time do you spend on your phone for non-work-related activities? How many hours do you watch TV after work each day?

There's no way around it: having your house in order requires making choices, establishing priorities, and sticking to disciplined routines.

It's time for some discipline.

CHAPTER 5

Health—Your #1 Priority

> *"The first wealth is health"*
> —Ralph Waldo Emerson

I usually receive about two calls per quarter from executives who ask me if I know a service that can help them pass a drug test. *"Not for myself, of course. I'm asking for a friend."*

Of course.

Apparently, many top-level decision-makers, including those in companies whose products and services are directly linked to pivotal areas of public safety, can only cope with the excruciating pressures of their careers through red-listed substances. It's really scary if you think about it.

I never realized how common top brass drug abuse was until, as part of my research for this book, I spoke to physicians and mental health practitioners. One of them is a counselor in an exclusive addiction clinic where outpatient services run upwards of $50k per month. Another runs a physician practice with a team of doctors who travel around the world by private jet to luxury hotels, yachts, and personal residences where they discretely, away from the public eye, manage the excruciating process of getting people off hard drugs.

When I asked about their clientele, both responded, *"Surgeons, lawyers, government officials, and high-profile corporate executives."*

Fun times.

Since the first wealth is truly health, it made sense to lead with it in the second part of this book which focuses on developing the fundamentals for sustainable career growth. Without our health we have nothing. Like time, we can't buy it with money, and once it's gone, we are finished.

The truth about executive careers is that they are incredibly physically demanding. The days are long, stress levels are high, senior leaders are on-call 24/7, and they can rarely fully disconnect. Extensive travel across time zones takes a toll on the body. Maintaining a balanced diet, a regular sleep schedule, and carving out time for physical activity requires extreme discipline. Top performers understand the importance of prioritizing their physical and mental health—not only to stay healthy and resilient for their own sake, but because at that level, optics matter as well.

Some may not appreciate hearing what I'm about to say next. To be clear, I support a more accepting attitude toward people from all backgrounds, shapes, and sizes as a society. The world needs more tolerance. At the same time, medical experts remain largely aligned on what is healthy and what is not.

Many of our top-brass clients receive extensive medical screenings as part of their executive benefits package. No one has ever told me that after their checkup, the doctor said, *"Sir, you're fifty pounds overweight, but don't worry, you're handsome."* Instead, they'll come back and say, *"I was told I'm fifty pounds overweight and have an increased risk for diabetes, heart disease, and other health issues, and that I need to take better care of my health."* No surprises here from a medical perspective, handsome or not.

There are many valid health-related reasons why people can't prioritize their physical or mental wellness the way they might want to. However, I would argue that most able-bodied people who neglect their health *know it* and simply haven't made the decision to take action yet.

The bottom line is, corporate executives find themselves under the microscope of the public eye and understand that vitality and optics matter for getting ahead. They also recognize that it's in their personal best interest to stay in good shape. Being their best, whatever that means for each person (optics aside), takes effort and discipline, just like everything else in life, and they make it a priority.

Taking care of our health pays dividends, and so does cultivating quality relationships and interests outside of work. According to the U.S. Surgeon General's Advisory on the Healing Effects of Social Connection[4], a lack of meaningful relationships not only poses a significant threat to our individual and societal well-being, but it also doesn't help with your career.

Boss-Minded Leaders Challenge the Status Quo by Asking Themselves:

▶ Am I making my health a priority?

▶ What aspects of my health am I neglecting—sleep, exercise, diet, or mental health?

▶ Do I want to make a change, and if so, how can I start with small, sustainable steps?

▶ What resources do I need to succeed? Should I engage professional help, or would it be beneficial to find a coach or accountability buddy?

CHAPTER 6

Live Big—Build Bonds, Expand Your World

"Friendship is the highest degree of
perfection in society."
—**Michael de Montaigne**

While the following quote is slightly exaggerated to make the point, we often hear comments like this from executives in transition who come into our practice. Many find themselves as free agents for the first time in their lives. When they realize that re-entering the market takes longer than expected, they soon discover they have no idea who they are outside of work or what to do with themselves during this downtime.

"For the last ten years, I've done nothing but bust my behind for Fun Times Corporation. I haven't taken vacations, never fully disconnected, had no time for hobbies, my friends were all from work, I don't really know my kids, and my partner and I have grown apart. I'm not even sure who I am anymore, what I like, or what to do with myself. I literally feel lost and I'm spiraling."

While beating ourselves up in hindsight about decisions we made based on the information we had at the time is rarely helpful, the frustration is understandable. However, there is a lesson to be learned here.

When our entire identity is wrapped up in who we are professionally—whether a Marketing VP, CFO, BU President, or CEO—things can become challenging when the one thing that holds our identity together, *work*, falls away. If 'all you are' is a CEO and, suddenly, you're not, then who are you? What's left for you to fall back on? What activities bring you joy, expose you to new ways of thinking, and offer support when work temporarily dries up? How and where will you combat loneliness, and find community, comfort, and support?

People whose identity is entirely consumed by work often have a reputation of being bland and one-dimensional. They're not usually the favorites around the water cooler because they're—rightfully or wrongly—perceived as boring for lacking a personal life.

Aside from the fool's errand of basing your entire inner stability on external factors like work, money, and status, since these can eventually become fleeting, doing so is also unhelpful for you professionally.

In the executive world, especially, personality carries weight. People are drawn to interesting individuals. Having a life outside of work helps counterbalance psychological fragility and isolation during life's rainy days and makes you a more well-rounded and engaging person to your network, teams, peers, and superiors.

If you want to think about what's best for yourself first, enriching your life with joy will pay far more long-term dividends than money. Apparently, nobody looks back at the end of their life wishing they had worked more. Looking at the Gallup numbers from that angle, I believe it. When our time runs out, what seems to matter most is the time we spent with those we loved, with ourselves, and in the activities and connections that brought us joy.

Side note: Hopefully, you make wise decisions about the people you choose to support you. I once got a call from a Corporate General Counsel who wanted to know how to get on corporate boards. When I asked him about his motivation, his flat response was that he needed the money. Given his current position and the caliber of the company he worked for, this gave me pause. He filled the silence by adding, *"I'm with wife number five, and the alimony is killing me. I need more income; the financial stress is impacting my work."*

People often say, *"as you make your bed, so you lie in it."* In the context of career performance, I would, perhaps a little flippantly, argue—based on anecdotal insights on my clients' often juicy personal lives—that *"how well you perform depends on with whom you lie in bed."* Whom you marry matters.

Bottom line: Leaders whose private lives are a hot mess typically won't deliver their best work or reach their full potential as quickly as those they compete with. Have some interests and passions, please. Surround yourself with good people. Harry, a technology executive and friend of mine, once said, *"I've always believed that there's room for levity in careers."*

I couldn't agree more. Having a good-natured personality and being fun to be around will take you far, especially at the top, where many tend to bury their personalities. Standing out in a positive way helps elevate your profile.

Being in good financial shape is another area where you want to have your house in order, in case something goes sideways—because it often does.

Boss-Minded Leaders Challenge the Status Quo by Asking Themselves:

▶ Am I making time for activities that bring me joy?

▶ Do I have a healthy circle of supportive people I can trust?

▶ Do I want to expand my social life? If so, how can I start with small, sustainable steps?

CHAPTER 7

Financial Discipline—Save More, Stress Less

"A penny saved is a penny earned."
—Benjamin Franklin

Some lessons must be learned the hard way. Here's a situation that's more common than you might think when executives come into our practice after an exit: money challenges, particularly after unexpected terminations.

Jane, a CMO who recently found herself out on the street after the new incoming CEO cleaned house, shared her frustration: *"I'm so stressed about cash right now. Dave and I sold the Aspen house, and we're pulling the kids out of private school. It's awful. I never expected to be in this position because I never expected to be fired. Absurd in hindsight, obviously—I've terminated so many people myself during my career! I should have planned for the fact that it could happen to me too. I think I just realized, I'm not that special."*

While senior executives often receive personal support with financial planning as part of their executive package, a staggering number still live paycheck to paycheck because they overstretch and spend a little too carelessly. After all, there's always more coming in, right? Annual bonuses, stock vestings... the never-ending money tree just keeps shaking off the dollars. *Until it doesn't.*

In my observation over the years, a significant number of executives view losing their jobs the same way most people view the possibility of running into major health issues: it only happens to other people. Ignorance is bliss. They often say, *"I never saw it coming!"* But ignoring the harsh realities of life and assuming that tough things only happen to others doesn't change what most leaders already know deep down: executive positions have a shelf life. Preparation and financial reserves are far better than the stress of remortgaging the house.

I don't mean to minimize the often-difficult realities of working families, but I would argue that financial planning is crucial, and many people aren't fully leveraging their potential to build reserves. I'm no Warren Buffet, but my recommendation would be to have twelve to eighteen months' worth of accessible funds in the bank, just in case an executive search process takes longer than expected—something that happens more often than not.

Speaking of time.

Boss-Minded Leaders Challenge the Status Quo by Asking Themselves:

▶ Am I making responsible financial decisions that will provide stability and peace of mind even during economic down-times?

▶ Do I need help in this area?

CHAPTER 8

Time Management—Own It

*"Time is the most valuable thing
a man can spend."*
—Theophrastus

When Anna, a client of ours, sat in her exit interview after resigning from a major tech company, the HR Director asked her why she quit her job. Worn out from four years of grinding it out across time zones and a *"damn bloody"* ungrateful boss, she shared, *"I felt like I had to work all the time and it was never enough. I'm burned out and want to find myself a company where the work-life balance is less shitty."*

According to Anna, her statement was not met with the empathy she had hoped for. The HR Director, who had somehow managed to survive ten years with the company, flat out told her, *"I'm sorry you feel that way. Every organization will take twenty-four hours of the day from you—if you let them. It is your job to establish healthy boundaries, manage your time, and negotiate the scope of your workload with your leader.*

If you haven't learned that with us, hopefully you will with your next opportunity."

Ouch.

It's not easy to defy today's 24/7 work culture, especially in hierarchical environments filled with power dynamics and peer pressure. Much could be said about our 'always on' culture and the over-obsession with work, but what good does it do? Top-level executives are legitimately expected to be always on, and they should (hopefully) negotiate highly competitive compensation packages to make this sacrifice worthwhile.

Knowing many leaders who have successfully figured out how to play the game, admittedly sometimes by appearing to work more than they actually do, I've witnessed firsthand that achieving a work-life balance is possible. At the end of the day, all of us must learn to be stewards of our life's clock, set boundaries, and find efficient ways to delegate work to get it all done. The alternatives are being a company doormat with no backbone and no personal life or to work at a gas station where there's no work to take home. Essentially, those are the options.

Authority and peer pressure aside, one of the hardest parts of self-management is maintaining consistent discipline in time management. Since we can't create more time, you'd think we'd be more motivated to improve in this area. Sometimes leaders complain that they don't have the capacity to implement everything this book recommends. And yet, others have managed to do it quite effectively.

There are many books written about time management, so I won't dive too deep into the 'how.' However, I will share the five top strategies that I consistently see successful senior executives use, aside from effective delegation.

Blocking time for focus work and value-generating activities

Some of my clients have this down to an art, but it involves 'training' their teams and superiors, and then being diligent about not caving. Leaders with strong boundaries and high productivity block time for focus and strategic work, then hold the line, allocating a couple of hours, a morning, or even an entire day. Their out-of-office notification is on, they close all communication channels, and shut down their email—sometimes even their phone. Uninterrupted time is crucial for getting things done quickly because the brain can't constantly switch between tasks without losing productivity.

Excellent email management

One client of ours always says she refuses *"to be a bitch to my email."* She explained, *"At some point, I no longer wanted the anxiety of waking up to 100+ emails every day. Plus, it was unproductive. So, I implemented a morning status meeting to address every issue when someone needed help, find a solution within the group, and then send them on their way. It saved me easily five to seven hours per week, which I spent on the golf course during the fabulous COVID work-from-home era."* Nice.

Eating the frog

Highly productive people make it a habit to tackle their most difficult and uncomfortable tasks first. This helps them avoid the procrastination trap and its draining effects on both productivity and emotional energy. The method is explained in the short and fun book by Brian Tracy, *Eat that Frog! 21 Great Ways to Stop Procrastinating and Get More Done in Less Time.*

Standing meetings

Some of my leaders have implemented standing meetings to reduce wasted time. Not only is standing healthy, counteracting the detrimental effects of our overly sedentary lives, but the change in posture—and the fact that most people want to sit down again—accelerates decision-making. Instant time back!

Personal time boundaries

Many successful, well-balanced, healthy, and happy leaders attribute their success to taking time away from work and making themselves completely unavailable. This involves trusting their teams and realizing the world won't end if they're not at everyone's beck and call—whether it's a two-hour blackout period, a full day, or an unplugged week of vacation without checking email. If we look at our European counterparts, it's certainly possible. The only reason we don't do it in the U.S. is because we often feel uncomfortable setting healthy boundaries. It's a choice.

Boss-Minded Leaders Challenge the Status Quo by Asking Themselves:

▶ How much time could I realistically free up for work or personal activities if I spent less time on social media, delegated better, or said 'no' more often?

▶ How could I re-invest that time, and what would I gain?

▶ What's stopping me from doing that?

▶ Do I want to make a change? If so, how can I start with small, sustainable steps?

▶ What resources do I need, or who do I need to set new expectations and boundaries with?

Maximizing Returns and Protecting
Your Downside on the Way In

This is where the rubber meets the road for leaders who want to not only increase access to new opportunities but also elevate their earnings potential and safeguard their downside.

In the following section, we will explore considerations around timing your job changes, navigating executive search at the upper echelons, why lining up legal support should be the new normal for your next executive transition, and critical negotiation areas to maximize your total compensation and protect your assets.

Just in case you bark up the wrong tree or business conditions change, causing the next opportunity to not work out as planned.

CHAPTER 9

When to Stay, When to Go—Timing Your Career Moves

"It's not always about speed;
it's about timing."
—Anonymous

Leon, a C-level executive from the defense industry, once told me, *"With almost every mistake I made in my adult life—and there were many—I looked back later and thought: I don't have a good feeling going into this. Whether it was working for a particular boss, accepting a job offer, trusting my superiors to look out for me, or my first marriage, I should have listened to my intuition. Today, I trust my inner voice much more and no longer try to rationalize it away. If something doesn't feel right, I pay attention and change course.*

Learning is part of life, so I don't beat myself up over past personal and professional decisions, but I know I could have saved myself and others from a lot of fallout if I had learned this lesson earlier."

Right place, right time. Timing is everything. There's some truth to both. Successful leaders like Leon, who reflect on how they maximized their careers, all have something in common—and it's not that their journeys were always linear, without peaks and valleys.

It is discipline, intuition, and planning. Hopefully, you've already done some baseline benchmarking on where you want to take your career and mapped out multiple avenues to gain the skills and experience you need to reach your destination.

Carving out top-level careers involves a lot of strategic thinking, changing course, and taking risks. The biggest decisions executives often ponder is how to make a move (internally or externally, vertically or horizontally) and when: now versus later. Patience, enjoying the process, risk-tolerance, and intuition are big factors in this deliberation. Once we learn to trust our inner voice, our gut rarely steers us in the wrong direction.

After hearing stories from hundreds of leaders over the years, two truths always emerge. First, more experience is always better than staying stagnant, which means it's wise to never rule out lateral opportunities as strategic stepping stones. Second, even if you're committed to your current company, it's worthwhile to keep an eye on the market and maintain a strong network. After all, you never know what might be around the corner or how the tide could turn internally.

Understanding that executive positions have a shelf life is another dynamic that should play into your timing evaluation. Knowing when it might be time to say goodbye is smart. Preparing to fly the nest could mean beginning a stealth search. Or, if for whatever reason the situation is challenging internally, it could also mean initiating a conversation with the company about a strategically facilitated (and incentivized!) exit. This is your opportunity to bow out gracefully—and with extra cash—before things really head south.

Either way, at some point, you may find yourself looking at the job market again. At higher levels, this will require new skills to effectively navigate the executive search process.

Starting at the director level, positions are less frequently posted. What does that mean for you? It means your job search now requires an entirely new level of resilience and skills in the planning, relationship building, and execution department.

The following pages will cover some key basics to remember and guide you on where to learn more about navigating this hidden world with confidence in the years to come.

Boss-Minded Leaders Challenge the Status Quo by Asking Themselves:

▶ Do I have clarity about my desired career path, and have I mapped out multiple ways to reach my destination?

▶ Have I been doing 'next level work' without title and pay? For how long? Is it time to start putting feelers out?

▶ Do I keep myself visible, both internally and externally, for suitable opportunities?

CHAPTER 10

Executive Search—What Top Players Know

"Commerce unites men."
—Charles de Montesquieu

If you ever thought, *I should find myself a head-hunter to help me find a job*, you have work to do. If you don't want to sabotage your access to future opportunities by the way you navigate the global headhunting and recruiting arena, you may want to dismiss some common misconceptions. If you're among those executives who 'get it,' feel free to skip this chapter and give yourself a big pat on the back.

It's surprising how many leaders rely on outside search firms to fill key roles on their teams—yet fail to recognize that these firms serve the corporation, not the candidate (you!).

Estimates vary, but many agree that 80-90 percent of executive jobs come from the 'hidden' job market, where top-level roles aren't publicly posted. At this level, companies often conduct searches confidentially—whether to manage timing, avoid rumors, or prevent stakeholder concerns.

Another striking fact: 70-80 percent of senior executives land their next role through their network. Given this—and the reality that companies often rely on agencies to fill top positions—building relationships with Partners, Practice Leaders, and Managing Directors at major search firms should be a core part of any leader's long-term strategy.

At the upper echelons, it's who you know that determines if you're on the map for new opportunities—or not.

A quick note on terminology: When I refer to recruiters or headhunters in this context, I mean those working at search firms like Egon Zehnder, Heidrick & Struggles, or Korn Ferry—not recruiters from corporate HR or internal Talent Acquisition teams.

Here are five key takeaways from ABREO's learning curriculum that we always emphasize to clients about executive search:

1. **The headhunter works for the organization that hires their firm to fill a role—not for you.** They also have the tools to find the talent their

corporate clients need, so they don't rely on networking with candidates. Their time is valuable, and it's wise to keep that in mind when reaching out.

Clients sometimes share their early-days mishaps in this space with us: *"When I started playing at this level, I used to send an email with my resume attached saying: 'Hi, so-and-so, I recently got laid off from my VP role at Fun Times Corporation. Can you help me find a new job?' No surprise, my response rate was zero."* Yeah. No kidding.

We usually end with a good laugh and some coaching on how to do better next time. Rejection is part of the process, but a personalized approach increases the chances of a response—laying the foundation for meaningful, mutually beneficial long-term relationships.

2. **Headhunters only have visibility into the roles their firm has been hired to fill**—they don't have a comprehensive view of the entire job market. They're not the unemployment agency. What does that mean for you? It means that you're well advised to build up your connections with several agencies.

3. **It's personal: the higher up you go, the more search becomes a relationship business.** Relationships take time to grow and mature. We advise building 'relationship equity' as early as the manager level and letting your network evolve with your career. Many tenured

executives maintain connections with 75+ global search firm contacts, tracked in a spreadsheet (like the free template you can claim as a thank you for buying this book). Over time, they've built genuine relationships with them. It's a labor of love, but as the saying goes—nothing ventured, nothing gained.

4. **If you're kind of a big deal, getting face time is easier.** That's just the way the world works. You'll get there.

5. **Consider your bottom line:** When it comes to your money it doesn't matter whether you're dealing with a corporate or agency recruiter. The hiring organization wants to maximize profit and pay you just enough so you won't head to the competition after a year or so.

Many recruiters and headhunters genuinely want to see you compensated well, but at the end of the day, their ability to influence your remuneration is limited. Some executives assume that because a search firm's commission is tied to their base salary (and sometimes their first-year bonus), recruiters have a vested interest in securing them the highest possible pay.

While that sounds logical in theory, if you do the math, you will see that the impact of, say, an incremental increase of $50K or $100K more for *you*, doesn't necessarily move the needle much for *them*. Plus, high-value perks like sign-on bonuses, stock options, executive housing, and severance packages, etc. won't impact their paycheck at all.

At the executive level, real wealth comes from long-term incentive programs. Since that pool of money doesn't affect a recruiter's paycheck, it's crucial to advocate for yourself rather than relying on external champions. In this world, everything always comes back to treating your career like a business, and watching out for your own P&L.

We routinely advise leaders that it is in their best interests to understand executive search in more detail. As such, we frequently recommend *Search in Plain Sight: Demystifying Executive Search* by Somer Hackley to clients who have blind spots in this area. It's a rare resource that pulls back the curtain on the agency world and is among the top-ranked books in its category on Amazon.

Most importantly it is full of tactical guidance and examples on how to navigate and build relationships with agencies, stay top of mind and in good standing, and avoid mistakes both during the search journey and the actual interview process.

Integrating relationship-building with executive recruiters into your long-term career strategy pays life-long dividends and will give you access to roles in the hidden job market. Knowing the right people matters.

This includes knowing a good attorney.

Boss-Minded Leaders Challenge the Status Quo by Asking Themselves:

▶ What missteps have I made with agency recruiters in the past due to a lack of knowledge?

▶ Am I ready to expand my understanding and start strategically building my network?

▶ Which executive recruiters do I already know, and how can I strengthen those relationships?

CHAPTER 11

Legal Support—Power, Protection, Leverage

"The best way to predict the future is to create it."
—Abraham Lincoln

For senior executives, this is often the case with the help of the right attorney.

Most professionals starting at the middle management level have legal support on their radar for unexpected exits. But at a certain level, it is also wise to engage Legal on the way in. This is important not only to specify exit-conditions up front (more on that later) but also, and especially, to avoid other unpleasant surprises hidden in the fine print of employment contracts. Take Shannon, a private client of ours—her experience is a pure gold teachable moment.

"After a tough year with my previous employer, I quietly started a stealth job search. After months of interviews, an opportunity finally came through. By then the relationship with my current company had deteriorated

so badly that I jumped on the offer and signed every-thing point blank because I was so desperate to leave.

Later I found out that I didn't just have to shut down my small consulting business, but I was also forced to resign my first two middle-market board positions that took me three years to secure. After I joined, the company cited for-mal policy and gave me no choice. That was bad enough, but what stung even more was realizing that several of my peers had successfully negotiated their ventures and board seats into their contracts. Needless to say, neglect-ing legal due diligence is a mistake I won't make twice."

For seasoned leaders at the VP level and above, it's common practice to have an experienced labor law attorney review their contracts, ensuring that both current and future employment, as well as outside earnings, are protected.

Typical points of contention include non-competes, side businesses or ventures, the ability to hold paid board seats, and defining exit scenarios that trigger severance provisions. Since this is a complex landscape, ABREO ensures every client understands key severance quali-fiers—equipping them to have an informed conversa-tion with their attorney. In this space, knowledge pays dividends and leverage matters.

We recommend setting up two or three meet-and-greets with experienced labor law attorneys to ask general questions and get a feel for the expert who will support you. It's crucial to understand the cost, process, required documents, and turnaround times upfront. If a law firm says their basic offer review takes two weeks, that likely won't work in a high-stakes, time-sensitive offer situation.

Note that you should not be charged for such an initial advisory session—this is the attorney's opportunity to earn your business.

Boss Tip:

Companies often offer stipends for executives. If you're negotiating an offer at the VP level or higher, you should ask if financial support is available to you.

Boss-Minded Leaders Challenge the Status Quo by Asking Themselves:

▶ Have I ever been caught off guard by contractual stipulations in the past?

▶ Do I have a trusted labor law partner to guide me through entry and exit negotiations?

▶ Which high-profile leaders in my network could provide a strong attorney recommendation?

CHAPTER 12

Negotiating Total Compensation & Exit Terms

"There are two times in a man's life when he should not speculate: when he can't afford it, and when he can."
—Mark Twain

One of the most vile and tragic transition stories I've ever come across is Tom's. If you've ever watched the TV show *Succession*—the critically acclaimed satire on toxic C-suite, corporate board, and family dynamics—you may remember the time when the character Tom was given the internal nickname 'Terminal Tom' during a low point on his path to power. His professional situation was so dire that it was likened to having 'cancer of the career.' Tom, the protagonist of this story, was a similar terminal case. Succession didn't have a happy ending. Sadly, neither did our Tom.

Tom was a Business Unit President who had spent nearly twenty years climbing the ranks at his company, making them a fortune along the way. When the board appointed a new CEO, Tom and his new boss didn't get along. Despite his vision and projected ability to take his BU even further, it was to no avail. Tom's career turned into a porta potty rolling downhill. While I don't know Tom personally in real life, the person who was involved in the case later described this story as *"one of the biggest professional shit shows"* he had ever witnessed throughout his career.

When the new CEO took over, he came in with a familiar playbook—bringing in his own people, as often happens in top-level shakeups. But there was one problem: Tom. Letting him go would come with a hefty severance payout, and there was no basis for a termination for cause. So, a plan was hatched. The strategy? Make Tom's life progressively more difficult until he resigned voluntarily, eliminating the severance expense altogether.

Tom loved his company and his teams, so much so that he didn't see the game being played against him. When they reassigned his reporting line, he chalked it up to business needs. When a territory restructuring stripped him of 25 percent of his P&L—and with it, a sizable chunk of his bonus—he stayed optimistic, believing things would course-correct. He was loyal. And blind to his new reality. With Terminal-Tom not taking the hint, upper management's patience began to wear thin. A new plan was curated.

Someone had a 'brilliant' idea—call a competitor and convince them to hire Tom! There was just one problem: they didn't have a role for him.

So, his employer sweetened the deal. A few well-placed incentives later, and suddenly, a position 'miraculously' appeared. Long story short, a sizable anonymous donation found its way to one of the competitor CEO's favorite charities, and just like that, Tom was off their plate.

You have to hand it to them, the way this entire deal was set up was pretty 'legit.' The new company didn't just let some lowly Specialist from their internal Talent Acquisition team handle this fake 'open position' but engaged a renowned search firm to make the entire thing airtight. Of course, the agency had no idea what was really happening behind the scenes.

When Tom received the poaching call from the search firm, he thought this was the best thing that had happened to him in a long time. He resigned, unwittingly handing his employer a double win: seven figures in severance savings and a tax write-off for their 'charitable donation.' He quickly signed the offer with the competitor, thrilled at his fresh start. The fact that nobody in the entire hiring process ever asked him if he had a non-compete with his existing employer to make sure the new company's legal bases were covered didn't raise any red flags with him.

Trusting as he was, Tom also overlooked his new employer's non-compete—still very much enforceable at the time. He also failed to pre-negotiate his severance. Having spent his entire career climbing the ranks internally, he wasn't sure how to approach it—and didn't feel comfortable trying. At this point he was just relieved to get out.

Six months later, his role was eliminated. Due to his short tenure, he walked away with a severance that basically bought him a gas station coffee and a book of stamps. To make matters worse, the non-compete he had signed with his new employer barred him from working for any major competitors for the next two years.

By his own estimate, his mistakes cost him over $3.5 million in lost earnings, severance, and market downtime. The whole ordeal stank to high heaven—but with no precautions in place, he had no recourse.

Seasoned executives who have been around the block a few times don't gamble with their wealth. Speculating and hoping for the best may seem like the trusting and easy route—until the fallout hits. Taking charge in this area can feel uncomfortable because money is deeply personal. For everyone.

Believe it or not, even most C-level executives get nervous when it comes to their own bottom line—even those managing massive P&Ls or overseeing vast sums of money. But the upside of negotiating is undeniable. Leaders who take charge in key areas like total compensation, severance, and outplacement at exit unlock financial gains that compound over time.

Mastering these areas creates powerful synergies for building and protecting your wealth.

Total Compensation

Many books have been written about salary negotiation. Only you will know from your past experiences and comfort level if this is a skill where you need to expand.

I used to be surprised by how hesitant even senior leaders can be when it comes to negotiation. For me, someone who bootstrapped a career from pretty precarious circumstances, negotiating for top dollar was never a 'nice to have'—it was an economic necessity.

It took me a while to understand that it was my 'I have nothing to lose by asking' mindset that gave me maybe not necessarily the confidence but definitely the courage to always ask for more, simply because I didn't have the luxury to care what people thought.

I attribute my successes in employment contract negotiation—both for myself and for others—to that sort of mindset. Learning not to fear rejection has made me more money than any other skill I've developed. Because if you don't ask, the answer is always no.

While I no longer negotiate employment contracts for clients—given the conflict of interest with our outplacement work—I make it a priority to pass on this skill to help others achieve more.

At ABREO, we integrate one-on-one mock training for recruiter conversations and advanced negotiation strategies into our executive learning curriculum. Practicing in a safe environment is crucial for leaders to build confidence and maximize their outcomes.

You won't master negotiation by reading fifty books on the subject—it's a skill that must be tested and refined in real life. If you do just one thing, make it this: dare to simply ask for more (or to pay less). That single action will put you ahead of anyone still working their way through the negotiation section at the library.

Our top advice for those who struggle with negotiation? Start small. Practice in low-stakes, everyday situations. Nobody becomes a cut-throat employment negotiator overnight if the confidence to ask for more isn't there in the day to day.

You don't have to start with intimidating big-ticket items like real estate or cars. Begin with small, everyday opportunities—like negotiating at the grocery store—where rejection is nothing more than a minor bruise to the ego. These low-stakes situations serve as your training ground, helping you build confidence and strengthen your negotiation muscles so you're ready for bigger deals down the line.

Next time you're at the bakery ten minutes before closing—when they're about to toss out unsold inventory—try this: Tell them you were only planning to buy six bagels, then ask if they'd drop the price if you take a full dozen instead.

They might say no. So what? The biggest lesson for hesitant negotiators is that 'no' doesn't hurt. In fact, 'no' often starts the conversation.

When it comes to total compensation and perks, you have plenty of levers to pull. Beyond base salary, there can be annual cash and sign-on bonuses, deferred compensation, SERPs, stock options, educational assistance, extra vacation time, conference budgets, executive housing, generous relocation packages, elite memberships, healthcare and lifestyle perks, financial planning support, or spousal benefits.

At higher levels, perks can include company cars, private drivers, business-class travel—or even access to the company plane once you're really up there. And then, of course, there's severance and outplacement, which we'll get to in a minute

In the employment context, we routinely hear from C-level executives, especially those who manage large amounts of money, that not negotiating will hurt the personal brand. The psychology behind this makes sense: if someone is hesitant to advocate for their own compensation, it raises doubts about their ability to assertively manage company finances, negotiate with suppliers, or drive tough deals with clients.

This is not to say that employment negotiations never fall apart. Yes, some people might take offense when you ask for more. But risk is part of the game. At the end of the day, your chances of getting more increase dramatically if you simply dare to ask. Not asking always means no. I wish more people would just give it a try—because it's the fastest, easiest path to extra.

When it comes to compensation, market research is essential. If you negotiate blind, you risk leaving money on the table—a mistake that can cost you dearly over time. The compounding effect of failing to negotiate will significantly impact not just your salary but also your bonuses, 401(k), Social Security contributions, and long-term earnings potential.

The best way to stay on top of the market is by casting a wide net for reliable information. Friends in HR—especially those in Compensation with access to professional market data surveys—are pure gold relationships (pun intended).

Industry peers, headhunters, and recruiters also offer valuable insights, though not as in-depth as our savvy friends in Compensation. And don't forget about the

EDGAR database or SEC filings—if you're looking at publicly traded companies, all C-level and Board compensation is public record and available there.

Until you're playing at that level—whether just below the C-suite or targeting privately held companies— you'll need to dig a little deeper to ensure your research is buttoned up.

Bargaining is a muscle—one that strengthens with practice. Start small by simply asking for more, get comfortable handling rejection, and refine your skills over time as you work your way up to bigger wins.

Negotiation isn't just about building wealth on the way in—it's also about protecting what you've built on the way out.

Boss-Minded Leaders Challenge the Status Quo by Asking Themselves:

▶ Do I have a clear understanding of market compensation for my current and target roles?

▶ Have I built relationships with people who can provide valuable compensation insights?

▶ Does negotiation intimidate me? What low-stakes, everyday situations can I use to start practicing my negotiation skills?

> ### 🐘 Boss Tip:
> One aspect we always stress with our clients is that while the bulk of the negotiation happens at the offer stage, the way you handle the beginning of the interview process is just as important. When you join ABREO's executive client community, we'll coach you one-on-one to refine these skills. Before you know it, you won't even break a sweat when a recruiter calls.

Severance

It is easy to understand from Terminal-Tom's story why securing exit arrangements at entry is one of the most critical negotiation areas for senior executives.

I once had coffee with a female board director—a true pioneer who secured her first Fortune 500 Director seat back when the space was almost entirely dominated by men. Boldly, she said, *"I've never met an experienced male top executive who didn't secure his golden parachute upfront. Most learn to do it by their first VP or C-level role. The smartest executives aim to make money on the way out just as much as on the way in."*

The next time you hear a high-profile resignation wrapped in the usual rhetoric—'spending more time with family' or 'pursuing a new direction'—chances are the decision wasn't entirely voluntary. It is also likely a lot of money changed hands. For better or for worse, this could be you.

When business targets aren't met, someone usually has to take the fall. Other common exit triggers include shifting market conditions, post-M&A redundancies, and leadership shakeups at the top.

Experienced leaders know their positions are temporary. They know the risk of an involuntary exit—and the financial strain of a long job search. With that kind of runway, liquidity matters. They also know that lengthy legal disputes on the way out are painful, expensive, and often less profitable than stacking the deck on the way in.

Ironically, 'changing business conditions' can be a lucrative wealth-building opportunity. Wealth is typically built in three ways:

▶ **Making more**—through aggressively negotiated compensation packages.

▶ **Losing less**—by securing strong severance protections to cover your downside.

▶ **Double dipping**—landing your next role while severance checks are still coming in or during a lump-sum payout period.

That severance money can now be invested and put to work for you. Nothing is more rewarding than profiting from getting fired. At the end of the day, it's just business—and business is a game. Again: Games are fun.

Savvy incoming leaders know the game. They understand that their highest value to an organization is at the point of entry—when excitement is high, and leverage is strongest. That's why they capitalize on the positive momentum early. Setting yourself up for success in this space isn't just strategy—it's also a bit of an art.

Our clients frequently navigate both internal and external recruiting processes for roles where severance should be addressed upfront. First-time VPs, Presidents, and C-level executives often struggle with this—especially in internal promotions, where there's a valid concern about offending key stakeholders.

Regardless of whether the transition is internal or external, the right approach can pay tremendous dividends. The key is to normalize severance as a standard part of the negotiation—without coming across as untrustworthy or abrasive—and to integrate it seamlessly into the broader negotiation without stalling the process.

Tom's situation could have played out very differently had he been more informed—and bold—about negotiating his golden parachute. Every time a leader learns this lesson the hard way, hindsight regret hits hard. The realization is always the same: *I wish I had dared to try negotiating my severance upfront.* Or worse, *I wish I had known that was even an option.*

Feeling overwhelmed about this topic is completely normal when it's a new skill set. That's why ABREO helps clients understand and navigate this critical area in detail.

Ultimately, your attorney should guide you through the offer process, but you still need to know how to introduce severance professionally—and close the deal. Once you master this, you may secure a much bigger slice of the pie if the company is willing to play ball.

Boss-Minded Leaders Challenge the Status Quo by Asking Themselves:

▶ Have I truly covered my bases for all possible exit scenarios?

▶ What cautionary tales from others' exits should prompt me to level up and avoid the same mistakes?

▶ Do I have a trusted attorney who can guide me on severance and other critical contract terms when negotiating my next role?

Outplacement

Outplacement support is a perk that is often included in executive severance packages. The goal? To help departing leaders re-enter the market and secure their next opportunity more easily. Typically, this service is provided by firms like ABREO.

Negotiating outplacement support into your exit package is a smart move. Leaders who have spent years at the same company, especially those who rose through internal promotions, often struggle to navigate the complexities of the executive job market. They've been out of the game too long. And once they're back in, they quickly realize the game has changed.

As mentioned in the chapter on executive search, navigating high-level opportunities in the hidden job market is a completely different challenge. It demands a level of preparation that often exceeds leaders' capabilities—and, frankly, their discipline—especially after difficult terminations.

CHROs and Chief Legal Officers understand these challenges, which is why they choose ABREO. They see our exit services as more robust, offering a deeper level of support than other providers. We take the heavy lifting of market re-entry preparation entirely off the leader's plate, ensuring a smoother and faster transition.

Instead of a basic resume review, we completely rewrite the executive's document, aligning it with the client's next-level aspirations. If you've never been through this process with professional support, chances are you've spent entire weekends tweaking your own materials—only to still receive corrective feedback from recruiters, *if* they were invested enough to even give you feedback.

Leaders trust us because we know exactly which financials and metrics to highlight to elevate their visibility for high-profile opportunities. Our concierge support also goes beyond the basics of resume and LinkedIn optimization, offering more in-depth learning materials and one-on-one consulting on navigating executive search, interview and negotiation strategies, and securing severance deals with your next employer.

Quality support in this space typically costs upwards of $10K, so it's crucial to know reliable providers who specialize in executive transitions.

Whether you go through your HR department or have a provider in mind, be cautious of anyone who isn't focused on market re-entry for high-caliber candidates or refuses to provide examples of their work. As with everything, advocating for yourself and protecting your downside pays long-term dividends.

If you're hesitant about negotiating outplacement support, keep in mind that receiving quality transition assistance benefits not only you but also the company that let you go.

No one expects a leader to be happy about losing their job, but there's significant employer brand upside when executives reach the point where they can genuinely say, *"While I wasn't happy that my employment with Fun Times Corporation ended, I respect how they provided the best possible support on the way out."* That's more credit than most corporations will receive.

Boss-Minded Leaders Challenge the Status Quo by Asking Themselves:

▶ Does my company offer outplacement as an executive exit perk, and do they partner with an executive-focused provider?

▶ Do I know any former leaders who've gone through the process and can share insights on their experience and the service scope?

▶ If not, do I already know a reliable executive outplacement provider who will rewrite my resume and offer consulting support around executive search navigation, negotiation (both general and severance), and legal planning that I can pitch to my HR department?

Go Big and Go Home:
Owning Your Exit Like a Boss

Getting let go isn't exactly the most fun experience in the employment lifecycle. For most, it ends up becoming a moment of deep reflection and personal growth. It also shapes them into more empathetic leaders. Being fired is one of life's ways of teaching us about its peaks and valleys—and how to grow stronger from setbacks.

Careers are much like life: things rarely go smoothly all the time, so it's important to anticipate the ups and downs. In the following pages, we'll explore the obvious, and sometimes not-so-obvious, signs that the writing may be on the wall, why losing your job could actually be a good thing (yes, seriously), what to avoid when it happens, and how to get back on your feet.

Being asked to leave is a humbling experience. And while we're on the subject of humility and leaving, let's challenge some preconceived notions about corporate legacy.

You'll discover why it's time to toss that concept into the landfill, along with any other outdated career beliefs.

CHAPTER 13

The Writing on the Wall—How to Read the Signs

"That which does not kill us makes us stronger."
—Friedrich Nietzsche

A famous example of how little business loyalty and relationships matter was this public case of high-profile corporate drama back in 1998. Jamie Dimon, now the CEO of JPMorgan Chase, was once savagely asked to resign during an executive retreat weekend by his then lifelong mentor and CEO, Sandy Weill. This was back in their Citigroup days, after they had been working together for fifteen years.

It was a prime lesson of how quickly even the longest of relationships can turn sour. Or maybe it wasn't all so quickly? Looking back, when Dimon gave an interview to CNBC in 2020, he said, *"When I was fired from Citi ... I was totally surprised. I shouldn't have been. There were a lot of tell-tale signs, but I missed them at the time."*[5]

An uncomfortable reality of corporate life is that if you decide to join the game, not everyone will play by the rules just because you do. Robert Greene's *48 Laws of Power* is a national bestseller for a reason. Chances are, one, or even several people in your professional orbit, don't play fair; like it or not.

For those who genuinely try to do right by others, it's important to remember that almost everyone around you—especially those with the loudest 'we win as a team' rhetoric—often have their own agenda. People are always working toward something that benefits them first: more access to opportunities, money, power, influence, status, publicity, bigger divisions, or more resources.

If you can accept this as a fact of human nature, the blows, setbacks, and personal disappointments that are part of every professional journey will be easier to bear—especially the realization that you may, at some point, become collateral damage. That is, unless you've already stepped into the negative spotlight by somehow upsetting the wrong people.

Sonja, an HR Director and good friend of mine, always says, *"True advocates are hard to find. Don't trust too easily or too many. Motivations and alliances can shift quickly. That's not to say community and camaraderie aren't possible, but when push comes to shove, very few will go to bat for you. At some point, you're likely to get stabbed in the back by someone."*

Board directors we interviewed for this book agree. When asked about the attributes that contribute to great careers, they all highlighted the usual suspects: a growth mindset, openness to feedback, strong leadership and collaboration, hard work, conviction, strategic and innovative thinking, relationship building, and a willingness to take risks.

However, they also had plenty to say about the darker side of corporate life—slander, destructive politics, backstabbing, scapegoating, and other 'innovative' tactics used to shut down opponents.

When alliances shift or politics backfire, business conditions can change. Often, these changes lead to exits. And when they do, the writing is often on the wall long before it happens.

Getting yourself fired with aplomb is truly an art form. There is an article from the Harvard Business Review called "The Right Way to be Fired" that has remained an evergreen since 2001. Here are some HR fundamentals to keep in mind.[6]

Whether a termination stems from business reasons— like financial struggles, M&A-related redundancies— or performance issues, someone ruffling the wrong feathers, misconduct, gross negligence, or an incoming leader wanting to clean house, the proverbial shit rarely hits the fan out of nowhere.

With group layoffs, rumors often circulate well ahead of time. The same is true for individual exits.

Executives entrenched in corporate warfare or leadership shakeups typically have a strong sense of what's coming. Forewarning signs reveal truths we often try to ignore—until we can't. The bottom line is: your position's expiration date may be about to hit.

The signals are often easier to recognize when you know what to look for, as they're not always as obvious as receiving a negative performance review—or several. More subtly, signs like reduced face time with senior leaders, exclusion from critical meetings, deteriorating relationships, fewer responsibilities, reallocated territories or budgets, being asked to hire and train your own replacement, or receiving impossible tasks are all common red flags.

Additionally, Performance Improvement Plans (PIPs) are often a covert way to push employees out the door. In many cases, performance isn't the real issue. PIPs are frequently used as a tool to create a paper trail for a 'for cause' termination. For the company, this adds another protective legal layer, making it more difficult for you to challenge the decision if you believe you have a case. It's also a legal strategy to avoid unemployment claims.[7]

Once placed on a PIP, the road to improvement is tough—especially if the PIP was never intended to be rehabilitative. Many employees recognize this. When faced with a thirty-, sixty-, or ninety-day plan, some will genuinely try their best. Others will straight up ask for a severance package while quietly starting their job search.

Similarly, when executive coaching is introduced, it's not always a sign of good intentions. Despite the significant financial investment from the employer, it's not always offered with a rehabilitative purpose. More often than not, executive coaches are asked to subtly guide a leader out the door. This is a tremendous waste of time and resources that could be better spent on severance and outplacement support to help the employee transition.

Boss-Minded Leaders Challenge the Status Quo by Asking Themselves:

▶ Do I have a clear sense of what's happening in my organization, or is my intuition telling me something may be going on—either directed toward me specifically or affecting the company as a whole?

▶ Have I noticed any telltale signs, and do I have an impartial confidante to help assess the situation?

▶ Am I financially, legally, and relationally prepared to hit the ground running in the external market if something were to happen tomorrow?

CHAPTER 14

Fired? Good. You'll Thank Them Later

"There is nothing either good or bad, but thinking makes it so."
—**William Shakespeare**

"Corporate termination styles can vary greatly—from infamous mass layoffs over Zoom to the 'concierge treatment.' Often, it happens on a Friday afternoon, with IT access cut as the employee walks to the room where they'll hear the news—likely located near the exit for a quick escort out. In other cases, the news is delivered over the phone, with instructions not to return to the office, as is common in executive exits. Sometimes, it's even done offsite.

No matter how it happens—whether the former boss or Legal is in the room—it's always a difficult, uncomfortable experience for everyone involved. Most HR people and executives dread this part of their jobs. That's why we will often have an HR person handle the exit who doesn't know the employee that well or at all. It makes the emotional toll it takes on us a little easier. Even though it's tough for everyone, once the initial shock fades and

> *with time and hindsight perspective, many leaders come to realize that it was the push they needed to make a positive change."*
>
> Dennis, VP HR

From an anecdotal perspective, having supported exit scenarios in various capacities, the good news is that for many, a termination really is a 'good thing.'

With some time passing, usually after they find their next opportunity, many will tell us, *"It had to happen," "It was for the better,"* or even *"It was a relief, I hadn't realized how unhappy I was until after I was gone."*

If you watched *Up in the Air*, where George Clooney's character, Ryan Bingham, administers mass layoffs as an outsourced outplacement consultant, you might recall what he tells one of the terminated employees: *"Anybody who ever built an empire, or changed the world, sat where you are now. And it's because they sat there that they were able to do it."*

I don't condone the unempathetic delivery that made this tragic reality of corporate life so sarcastically memorable in the movie, but there's a grain of truth to it. While not everyone goes on to change the world as

Ryan suggests, for many professionals and executives, life post-termination improves—especially when they leave toxic environments.

Unfortunately, that hindsight realization doesn't ease the pain in the moment. Few people—unless they secured severance upfront, built significant financial reserves, and developed the Panta Rei mindset that this is just another part of life's ebb and flow—can simply shrug off a major blow like this. Since that *'doesn't matter – NEXT!'* attitude doesn't develop overnight, how can you best navigate through this experience when it happens?

It's completely okay to have an emotional reaction. Staying composed in this situation is tough, even if it was expected. Most HR professionals have witnessed the full spectrum of human emotions in these moments.

Understand that the decision has already been made, and no amount of pleading will change it. You can ask for the reason, but most likely, everyone in the room will be very guarded for legal reasons. If you do receive a sincere thank you for your service, consider it a kind gesture. Having heard many termination stories over the years, the lack of gratitude and basic decency is often what upsets people the most—especially after years of loyal service.

Since this is your final business transaction with the company, it's crucial to know how to handle it. Legal and HR professionals strongly recommend refraining from signing anything in the moment, regardless of how you feel—and especially if you feel pressured. Take the paperwork and avoid making threats or discussing any next steps. Simply tell them you'll get back to them. That's all they need to know for now.

Grab your personal items if you can (they might be mailed to you), leave without making a scene, and cry in your car. Then, take a moment to pat yourself on the back for making it this long. Take a deep breath and call your lawyer.

Ideally, you've already engaged them when securing your exit conditions on the way into the company and briefed them recently if you suspected an unfavorable event was coming. This way, they are up to speed and ready to assist.

Rejection is just a step in your path. Your future has much more in store for you.

Boss-Minded Leaders Challenge the Status Quo by Asking Themselves:

▶ If I suspect something may be in the works, do I have legal support lined up?

▶ Am I mentally prepared for when it happens?

CHAPTER 15

From Fired to Fierce—Your Comeback Playbook

> *"Our greatest glory is not in never failing, but in rising every time we fall."*
> —**Confucius**

"My advice for termination scenarios aside from never signing anything right away is: stay quiet and don't do anything rash afterwards. Stealing client information is always a classic. I also recall a Group CEO who downloaded the entire R&D database to an external hard drive, claiming it was his work product since he oversaw the function. If he had reviewed his employment contract, he would have known that argument doesn't hold up for most corporate work products. The key takeaway: don't do anything shady or criminal that could put you at risk for legal action or undermine your exit negotiations.

Also resist the urge to contact confidantes within the business. Keep your mouth shut and don't reveal your next move. For most people, this is difficult—they want to express their disappointment and frustration to people they know. But the reality is that anyone still inside the company is an adversary until the financial and legal matters are settled. Let the dust settle, see if you can cash out, and focus on your next steps. You must defer your need for empathy in this moment."

Josh, Corporate General Counsel

Dominating at exit like a boss means playing the business game at its highest level, which is why it requires legal support and discretion. It may not sound like fun, but with the right attitude, playing the game can bring significant upside.

Negotiating at Exit

If the golden parachute wasn't secured upon entry, this is the time to negotiate, regardless of what, if anything, was offered. In mass layoff scenarios, there's usually little room for negotiation since the budget has already been set. However, individual exits sometimes offer more flexibility. Many senior executives who have gone through this—often more than once—report that there is value in at least trying to negotiate. As we've discussed in previous chapters: if you don't ask, the answer is always no.

The amount of flexibility from the business depends on factors like the strength of the employee's case and the company's financial position. Credible labor law attorneys can advise on the best strategy and the likely outcomes in each situation—whether the goal is a quick settlement or preparing for a long, often exhausting court battle.

At the lower and middle management levels, employees often attempt to negotiate on their own, knowing that HR and Legal departments are eager for a quick close and the signature on the exit paperwork. However, legal support is always the recommended route. For those without legal expertise, navigating the complexities of non-competes, short- and long-term bonuses, stock vestings, and other payouts is nearly impossible on a good day—and even more so under emotional stress and financial duress.

Laying Low

Given how closely we often work with colleagues and confidantes, staying quiet can be difficult—but it's in your best interests. To protect the integrity of your exit negotiation, it's crucial not to speak with anyone in the company until everything is settled. While most colleagues mean well, they often struggle to refrain from gossip—even if they don't intend to sabotage your process. As Josh said, defer your need for empathy from the professional community.

Distance is crucial, not just for maintaining process integrity, but also for your emotional recovery. Take a moment to process the loss, then—depending on your situation with the company—prepare for the executive search journey as quickly as possible.

Understanding the Dynamic Has Changed

One of the hardest realities senior leaders often face during terminations is that their market value often decreases afterward. People begin to view them differently. Many are surprised by how few former colleagues will reach out, or how few industry peers will offer support or proactively assist with the job search once word gets out.

Understanding this dynamic can be a tough blow to the ego. It's similar to the downgraded status of a football player after a poor season. Leaders who didn't protect their emotional boundaries and over-identified with their colleagues as 'family' often have a particularly hard time when their former team stays silent. It stings.

Overestimating loyalty, the quality of connections, or former alliances is a common misconception. Many upper management professionals are accustomed to others catering to them due to their position of power. Once that power fades, people will quickly realign with the next powerful leader. There's a wise saying in Germany: *'Whose bread I eat, his song I sing.'*

Realizing the fleeting nature of loyalty can be tough to accept. While the disappointment is understandable, it's important to remember that people are not necessarily against you—they are just for themselves.

Acting with Urgency

Unless you've decided to step away from the corporate world or your career entirely, you'll likely want to re-enter the market as quickly as possible. There are three major mistakes we see in the market re-entry process: **delaying it too long, not being proactive enough, and failing to prepare properly.**

After many grueling years of corporate work, often while balancing significant family responsibilities, it's understandable that many leaders feel exhausted. When large severance sums are involved, it's common for people to simply want to take a break and step away from it all for a while.

At this stage, immediately pulling the plug and taking a six-month sabbatical is generally not advisable. At the executive level, a job search can take at least six to twelve months. If you're eager to get back into the saddle quickly, especially if you're concerned about finances, taking an extended break can be a poor decision. It often leads to sheer panic around the nine-month mark. Remember Jane's financial problems? If you don't take action, that could be you. Don't be Jane.

Diligent Preparation

We advise our clients to kick-start the search process as quickly as possible. Diligent preparation for market re-entry is the first step. Your resume and LinkedIn profile must be in top shape to capture the attention and advocacy of recruiters, headhunters, C-suite executives, and board directors.

Most executives are not equipped to bring their own documents up to the quality and financial standards required at that level. At ABREO, we apply a level of scrutiny that DIY products can't match. When six- or seven-figure total compensation packages are at stake, it makes sense to invest in your future by engaging a specialist.

The number one issue we address for our clients is positioning them as business leaders. For executives who don't manage a P&L or aren't in the CEO role, this can be a challenge. However, at your level, you're expected to think, project, operate, and quantify your impact financially. Especially for functional leaders, it requires a paradigm shift to assertively showcase your expertise and accomplishments with metrics and financials—which is much easier to do with the help of a professional.

Engaging Your Network

Once your resume and LinkedIn profile appropriately showcase your qualifications, accomplishments, and elevated executive status, it's time to get active. Remember, 80 percent or more of executive positions are sourced through your network. Taking action is key. Right now, your market value is down, and the longer you wait, the more time works against you. If you simply wait for the phone to ring, it could be a very long wait.

Many of our clients struggle with this, but you need to start reaching out. Let your network of headhunters, board directors, and other high-profile connections know you're looking for your next opportunity. It's part of the process, and there's absolutely no shame in that.

Hopefully you have stayed in touch over the years so you're not calling out of the blue asking for a favor along the lines of *"Heeeey…how's Tommy's baseball practice going? Oh yeah, that's right, it was soccer, my bad… Uh yeah, so anyways…. I know it's been a while, but I was wondering if you could do me a favor in case you hear something about open positions in…."* Please, no.

Many people neglect their connections while fighting through the day-to-day grind of their careers. But at the upper echelons, where relationships matter more than anything, you can't afford to let quality connections slip. If you want to tap into someone's generosity, you need to nurture the relationship along the way. Don't be the person who only calls when they need something.

Make an effort to stay actively engaged and in touch. Reach out every once in a while during the sunny days of life. Check in and remember what matters to people. Ask about Tommy's soccer practice, and treat professional relationships with a more personal touch—even if there's a transactional aspect to the connection. You'll find that if you approach people genuinely rather than just transactionally, most won't hesitate to lend a hand on a rainy day. Those are your people.

Once your house is in order and you've connected with everyone who might be able to help, *then* you can step back and take a break. After kickstarting your job search and informing critical stakeholders, you've set things in motion that will start working for you behind the scenes. *Now,* you can continue your efforts from the Bahamas.

Terminated executives have *one* opportunity to get market re-entry right. For those who struggle in this area, investing in support to develop a profile that meets the high standards of global headhunters and recruiters should be a consideration. It's also important to remember that C-level contacts and board directors in your network won't want to stick their neck out for you if your documents aren't in top shape. Don't ask for their help until your resume clearly demonstrates the financial impact of your work and your ability to influence business outcomes at the highest levels.

Prepare diligently, grind it out, be consistent, stay humble. The reward for your efforts will come.

Boss-Minded Leaders Challenge the Status Quo by Asking Themselves:

▶ In case I lose my job, do I have copies of my performance reviews, key metrics, and other relevant financial or operational impact information readily available?

- ▶ Have I received constructive feedback from headhunters or recruiters about my application materials that suggests I shouldn't go through the preparation phase alone?

- ▶ Am I about to enter the VP or C-level arena for the first time? Should I consider getting help to elevate my executive profile?

- ▶ Which relationships that I once valued have I let lapse? Who should I casually check in with or stay in touch with more frequently moving forward?

Don't Forget Your Bonus Gifts: Complimentary Executive Transition Resources from ABREO

If you haven't yet claimed your complimentary **Executive Transition Checklist & Communication Tracker**, now is the perfect time.

Whether you are about to embark on a stealth search or have just left your previous organization, navigating your market re-entry can be overwhelming. Since 80 percent of executive positions are sourced through leaders' networks, diligent preparation and effective stakeholder management are vital at your level.

Normally included in every ABREO executive service package, our Transition Checklist & Communication Tracker are now available as complimentary gifts exclusively for *Like A Boss* readers. These resources will help you stay organized during your preparation and keep track of critical conversations with high-profile stakeholders—not only for your upcoming executive search process but also for years to come.

To receive your gifts along with our quarterly publication, The Executive Club (unsubscribe at any time), visit:

www.theabreofirm.com/gift and provide your email address. **Page password: LABGift**

If you need additional support during high-profile market transitions, you know where to find us.

To your success and prosperity,

Elisabeth Constantin
ABREO Executive Services, LLC
Nashville, TN

CHAPTER 16

Canceling Yourself—Rethinking Corporate Legacy

> *"Care about what other people think and you will always be their prisoner."*
> —Lao Tzu

This lesson comes from one of our clients, Linda, a Finance Vice President. Linda was next in line to take over from her soon-to-retire boss, the CFO. Despite being groomed and built up for years—largely to make her boss look good—when push came to shove, the CFO didn't give Linda the vote of confidence as her successor.

Without going into too much detail, the CFO—who was the first woman ever to make it into the company's C-suite—wanted to maintain the image of an all-male executive team to protect her own post-retirement legacy. Her agenda was to preserve her relevance as not only the *first* but also the *only* female to ever break into the old boys' club by hiring a man to take her place.

While Linda eventually got her well-deserved CFO position, it wasn't without turmoil. The company went through an external search, only to later offer the position to Linda—just as they had planned all along. This process cost them a pretty penny, as the search firm obviously didn't do their 'due diligence' work for free. It was a classic missed win-win: the company could have saved money and frustration, Linda could have secured a larger bonus, and the departing CFO could have left without the reputation of being a bitch who doesn't help other women. *Facts.*

"Unless you were the founder of the company, the idea of corporate legacy should be completely discarded. Once you're gone, no one cares about the job you did yesterday or about you as a person. I've seen many leaders undermine their successors' chances by withholding endorsements or even actively sabotaging them to get them ousted. Typically, this behavior comes from a fear that the successor will make too many changes or course-correct in a way that eviscerates their legacy.

This is quite common, especially in executive retirement scenarios. When companies are convinced that the internal candidate is indeed the best choice, they often delay the search process or final decision past the incumbent's retirement date instead of putting their foot down. What ends up happening is often a waste of time for everyone involved—undignified and unbecoming really for a leader who should prioritize the organization's well-being over personal sentiments."

Josh, Corporate General Counsel

As humans, we all want to feel seen, heard, and appreciated. We seek meaning in our lives, knowing that we've contributed to something greater than ourselves. Our lives matter—to so many. Your life matters to many. The desire to shape your legacy is completely understandable.

As intelligent individuals, and with all we know about the fragile stability of corporate ecosystems, it should become clear that legacy and companies don't mix well together. Unless you built the business from the ground up, I would argue that the corporate environment isn't the best place for legacy-building efforts. A more realistic approach might be to focus on your immediate circle of influence—your family, friends, and community. But why not the corporate world, you might ask?

In the work context, your legacy will always be remembered not by the collective enterprise, but at the individual level. Corporations are, in and of themselves, empty shells. It's the people who make the company—your teams, mentees, colleagues, superiors, and even your adversaries, if you managed to earn their respect.

Businesses have no room for sentimental pastimes. Organizations must remain nimble, quickly adapting to rapidly changing market conditions and both internal and external pressures to maintain a competitive edge.

Who cares if you took the company public or outsourced tech support to India? They might decide to go private again in five years, or India could raise its talent costs, rendering your contributions irrelevant in an instant. The day your decisions are up for reversal in some sterile conference or boardroom, don't expect anyone to pause and say, *"But remember when Jack worked so hard to get this deal pushed through?"* Please, no.

This realization can sting after years of hard work and emotional commitment. If letting go of legacy is tough, it might help to remember that everyone who knew you will eventually be gone too. In time, there will be no one left to remember you. Knowing that the shadow of your so-called legacy will be fleeting and short-lived, why bother in the first place? So much good can be done in other areas of life where your impact can be felt for much longer.

Work will always be work. If you asked John and Jenna about leaving a legacy in work environments, they would respond with something like, *"Who cares?!"* I know that for a fact because I asked them. I would also argue it's a pretty healthy way to look at things considering that everything changes, and nothing ever stays the same.

There's another reason why corporate legacy thinking is rarely in people's best interests: it limits our ability to think critically. Legacy focuses on how we will be remembered, or more specifically, how others will perceive us. While it's true that everyone has to people-please their way through corporate life to some extent—after all, there's always someone with the power to chop your head off (C-level boss, CEO, the board)—legacy thinking often clouds our judgment.

If someone is solely focused on how they'll be remembered after they're gone, will they be able to prioritize what's best for the business over their own personal ambitions?

Ego-driven decision-making is rarely good practice, in business or in life. If we apply this to our CFO succession example, it's clear that her self-centered objective wasn't just detrimental to the company—costing them more time and money—but also to her own reputation and exit.

When ego takes over, it becomes difficult to recognize lucrative opportunities, both externally and internally. Leaders—especially those from older generations or those navigating rocky waters within their organization—can become so focused on what they leave behind that they miss the window to cash out. Being strategic about leaving might involve initiating a conversation about a planned, incentivized exit with the company before you overstay your welcome and the tide shifts.

Missing the window to leave on a high note could result in a significant loss. Leaving with your head held high, extra cash in your pocket, and celebrated for your accomplishments—with dignity intact—will likely be a far more lasting and positive memory for everyone involved than clinging to a fleeting concept of legacy.

Your career is a business until the very last day. Taking a final hit to your personal P&L at the end would be a real shame. Do you want to find yourself asking the difficult question: Have I learned nothing? You're smarter than that.

Boss-Minded Leaders Challenge the Status Quo by Asking Themselves:

▶ How do I feel about letting go of the idea of corporate legacy?

▶ Do I know leaders who've put their ego aside regarding retirement or other exits? What can I learn from them about the attitude and mindset of treating a career like a business?

▶ If I let go of this, where do I want to redirect my legacy focus? Who and what truly matters to me?

Next Level Gravitas:
Diversifying Your Executive Presence

Nepotism aside, top executives typically reach the summit by doing more and cultivating a broader network of relationships. These individuals add value beyond their day jobs, creating powerful synergies that unlock additional visibility and opportunities.

In the following section, we will highlight the most common accelerators for executive careers: public speaking, board service, and academia.

While these avenues offer significant potential to expand internal and external status, accelerate the path to the C-suite, and provide personal enrichment, many busy executives find it difficult to add them to their plate. This is where those who are truly committed to reaching the top go the extra mile, contributing beyond their current scope of responsibilities.

They also understand that establishing themselves in these areas can open up lucrative alternative professional avenues—whether they need to pivot quickly after an unexpected exit or as a rewarding path after their corporate career.

The takeaway here is this: carving out access and visibility offers high rewards, but it takes time. The key to success in these areas is to bite the bullet and shorten the runway by starting *early*—working on these pursuits *in parallel* with your corporate career.

CHAPTER 17

Own the Stage—Build Your Speaker Profile

*"All the great speakers were bad
speakers at first."*
—Ralph Waldo Emerson

Things once took an interesting turn when a Fortune 100 company asked us to prepare their Chief Information, Data, and Security Officer for market after a separation. When we started working with Toni, she was in the final stages of completing her first business book. Over the past couple of years, Toni had been building her public profile through speaking engagements and panel appearances at industry conferences. So, when her book was released, she launched from an elevated starting position.

When we checked in with her a few months later to see how her corporate job search was going, she said, *"Oh, that's on hold. I'm making good money as a consultant now that the book is out, and I'm focused on speaking engagements and seminars. I might stay on this train for a while and see where it takes me."*

> Sometimes, you never know where the next pay-
> check will come from, but stories like these always
> show: when you put things in motion, unexpected
> doors and opportunities can open up.

Many people believe they need to publish a book to build a speaker profile. While it's true that people take that route, it's not necessary. It's also not necessary to wait until you are further along in your career to start your public speaking journey. Waiting too long is a mistake.

In their thirties and forties, many leaders feel insecure about public speaking or mistakenly believe they have nothing valuable to share. Personally, I've never met an established executive who didn't have something substantial to offer as an expert in their field.

Similar to building a board career after retiring from corporate life, delaying the establishment of your gravitas as an industry expert is the old way of doing things. If you want to shorten the runway and get ahead of the curve, taking action earlier is the best path to success.

I would argue that building conference and speaker visibility should start organically as early as the senior specialist level—so, really *quite junior*. Why? Because at that stage, few people dare to put themselves out there by actively seeking opportunities to get involved. Those who do, however, instantly stand out.

Building organic relationships for public speaking opportunities at a younger age also beats paying for expensive reputation management services later to pitch you to media platforms, etc. Conference organizers are often grateful for fresh faces and boots-on-the-ground operational perspectives—it's a welcome change from seeing the same people at every event. If you're not actively putting yourself out there yet, consider doing so once you reach the manager level. That's when savvy professionals start negotiating conference budgets into their employment offers. And if you're already traveling to an event, you might as well level up and get involved.

Much of this is about relationship building and playing the long game. If you stay hidden in your office fifty-two weeks a year, with no one knowing who you are or the great work you do, it's unlikely you'll get a call out of the blue asking you to share your expertise publicly. Again, it all comes down to visibility. So, where do you start?

There's no one-size-fits-all recipe for carving out a path to public speaking. Most people network their way into it, gradually building from there. The next time you attend a conference, why not reach out to the organizers or panel moderators and ask for some face time? If you're in Finance, you might be a member of organizations like Finance Executives International (FEI). If you're in Human Resources, perhaps you're with SHRM. These groups often host learning and networking events for their members; excellent opportunities to engage in panels or local roundtables.

Once people volunteer a few times, they typically build a speaker bio. This one- or two-page document briefly outlines your background, areas of expertise, and, once you've accumulated a few engagements, a list of recent conferences and events where you've spoken. A speaker bio is an excellent way to market yourself, giving conference organizers an immediate sense of who you are and what you bring to the table.

As you're starting out, you'll likely need to actively chase organizers and stay on top of it for a while. But once you break in, perform, and deliver on stage, you'll likely get called again—especially if you nurture those relationships. Each time you build your experience as a speaker, your engagement list and network grow with you. People will take notice, not just within your industry, but also internally. Your expert reputation will grow when others see you're in demand for public speaking.

Always remember to express gratitude for every opportunity and send a thank-you note. Never make the mistake of becoming arrogant, thinking you're 'all that and a bag of chips.' While expertise is valuable, entitlement has no place. At the end of the day, conference organizers will call back the participants they liked and who were easy to work with during the preparation phase.

Building a speaker profile is a great way to get on the map for other professional opportunities and expand your network. Elevating your network is particularly important if paid board service is a long-term goal for you.

Boss-Minded Leaders Challenge the Status Quo by Asking Themselves:

▶ Have I considered asking for a conference budget?

▶ What topics would I feel comfortable speaking on, perhaps starting with a panel?

▶ How do I feel about reaching out to conference organizers before or during an industry event to build relationships and offer my active participation?

▶ Who in my industry has an established speaker profile? Is my relationship with them strong enough that they might eventually make introductions to help me get in the door and on stage?

CHAPTER 18

Fast-Tracking Your Board Career—Start Early, Lead Strong

"Start by doing what's necessary, then do what's possible, and suddenly you're doing the impossible."
—**Saint Francis of Assisi**

True story about what happens when people think grinding it out is beneath them (hint: not much). During one of my speaking engagements at a Harvard Club on maximizing career ROI in high-profile job transitions, a distinguished executive raised his hand and asked a question about finding his first board seat.

"I don't understand it," he said. *"I've been in public company C-suites for the past ten years. I'm the perfect board candidate. I even read a book about what makes a good director candidate and I match the profile. Why is nobody calling me? It seems impossible to get there."*

I asked if he had invested in formal credentialing and notified his undoubtedly high-profile network that he was actively seeking these types of opportunities.

He looked at me like I had lost my mind. *"Well, of course not,"* he said. *"I don't need to put myself out there in that way. Leaders of my caliber want to get poached."*

I let it slide and let the audience deliver the reality check. Tenured board directors in attendance were quick to offer a different perspective—not only on the necessity of networking but also on the importance of investing in credentialing and learning first.

Someone spoke up and said, *"You need to get credentialed. Board work is a serious profession; it's a whole other set of letters up there. The next thing is you need to network. In that order. If someone wants to connect with me about getting on my radar for board work, the first thing I ask is whether they've done their work in learning and credentialing. If the answer is no, I'll end the conversation quickly. Those are not serious people. Do the work, then network. But you must do both, because for most people, the phone isn't going to ring out of the blue."*

Bottom line: do more, and don't impose on people's busy schedules until you can demonstrate you mean business.

For many senior executives, serving on a corporate board represents the pinnacle of their distinguished careers. The director community almost resembles a secret society—you don't hear or see much of them, but they hold tremendous influence over what we eat, consume, how we spend our time, and how much we pay for it all. When you consider their influence, public company directors are some of the most powerful people in business and society, which is why these positions are so highly coveted.

Additionally, this path offers a wide range of benefits, including enhanced prestige, the opportunity to lead without being bogged down in the operational weeds, and substantial financial rewards. Board service also often serves as a stepping stone to CEO positions. Having a solid understanding of boardroom dynamics and governance can help first-time CEOs immensely fast-track their success in both public and private company C-suites. Naturally, executive search firms recognize this, treating board experience as a key differentiator in succession stress testing and external searches.

The sobering reality first: there is more demand than supply for board director roles. In the United States, it takes an average of one to five years to land the first paid position. How's that for popping your bubble of lofty ambitions and hopes for an easy payday?

Beating the Clock

The good news is that there are ways to shorten the runway, primarily by starting this journey early rather than waiting for retirement, as many older generations have historically done. Typically, after a year of playing golf and with the spouse hinting that life was somehow better when they weren't 'around so much,' board work starts to appear on the radar. At this point, however, you're late to the party. Very late.

In today's rapidly changing world, where boards seek dynamic and diverse leadership, retirees with a significant gap since their last position are not considered prime candidates. More often than not, they've been out of the operational game for too long.

This is great news if you're younger. Starting your board search earlier—such as when you're at the Director or VP level—gives you a higher likelihood of beating the clock, breaking in, building your portfolio, and working your way up. That way, when you eventually retire, you're not starting from scratch. Of course, bringing the right experience to the table still matters.

While qualification requirements can vary, the traditional heavy-hitters—such as distinguished CEOs, CFOs, and other C-level executives—remain highly sought after. A competitive board profile typically includes expertise in key areas like finance, strategic P&L responsibility, driving growth at scale (both nationally and globally, depending on the board's and company's needs), economic turnarounds, mergers and acquisitions (M&A), and initial public offerings (IPOs), just to name a few. Additionally, leaders with deep functional expertise, particularly in fields like Technology, Risk, and Data, are increasingly in demand as boards seek specialized knowledge to make informed, long-term decisions.

As mentioned, the most recommended way to get started and beat the clock is through education.

Education

It's clear that the route to board service is largely about access and visibility. If you want to get on a board, being educated about board service is the best substitute for not yet having any experience.

Starting with reading about boards is an excellent way to familiarize yourself with the different types of boards, understand what makes a competitive candidate, and determine if this is a path you truly want to pursue.

You'll find that privately held companies, middle-market organizations, family businesses, PE companies, and startups offer numerous opportunities to get involved and build your portfolio. A list of low-stakes resources to help kickstart your learning journey is included at the end of this book.

If you decide to get serious, we recommend investing in an official, ideally accredited, board director certification. Many Ivy League universities offer prep courses, which, while prestigious, don't always come with a credential or access to established directors. The main credentialing body in the United States is the NACD—the National Association for Corporate Directors. Not only do they provide education and formal certification, but more importantly, they grant access to a national network of established directors.

While the phone won't just ring with an offer simply because you've obtained formal accreditation, respected and established directors agree that education and gaining access to the broader director community is vital for your relationship building efforts. This is why NACD is widely considered the top choice for aspiring directors.

Engaging your Network

This piece is pretty simple: if directors, CEOs, and C-suite executives in your network don't know that you're looking for these kinds of engagements, you won't be on their radar. If you're not on the radar, you'll never be top of mind when opportunities come up through the grapevine.

By managing relationships the right way and consistently—perhaps with the added boost of high-profile industry speaking engagements or visibility in academia—you'll stack the deck in your favor, growing a larger, higher-quality network. Visibility breeds opportunity.

Professional support is also available if you choose to go that route—either through established search firms (another reason to build out your search firm network) or specialized board placement agencies. The latter typically charges a substantial fee for their active support in trying to place you. However, with approximately 80 percent of board roles found through networks[8], paid agency support can be an additional pillar, but it is usually not recommended as the sole route to success. Seasoned directors generally agree: there's no shortcut for rolling up your sleeves and putting yourself out there.

> **Boss Tip:**
> Credentialing and memberships can sometimes be negotiated as perks covered by the employer. Additionally, for certain companies, board service can serve as a promotion and retention tool, allowing employers to retain critical talent when internal progression paths have been maximized.

Boss-Minded Leaders Challenge the Status Quo by Asking Themselves:

▶ Do I want to learn more about board service and invest in low-stakes learning through books and other resources before diving deeper?

▶ Who in my network holds board director positions and might be open to a conversation with me, without feeling like I'm wasting their time if I'm not credentialed yet?

▶ Would my current employment contract permit paid board positions, or would it require a conversation for approval?

▶ Does my company cover the cost of credentialing, such as through the NACD?

CHAPTER 19

Serving in Academia—Making an Impact Beyond Business

"The first half of my life I went to school, the second half of my life I got an education."
—Mark Twain

At a certain point in their careers, senior executives often ask themselves *"What's next for me?"* After spending decades in corporate environments, many find teaching to be a refreshing prospect, and an opportunity to continue their own journey of life-long learning.

Whether driven by corporate burnout, a desire to give back, a wish to relive the invigorating campus experience of their younger years, or the need to secure a Plan B for their long-term exit or retirement strategy—many executives have academia on their radar. And they are in demand!

Students are eager for wisdom, especially that which comes from hands-on experience and leadership. Executives are a huge asset for universities, bringing decades of real-world expertise to their teaching and adding a practical component that goes beyond theory.

Getting boots on the ground in academic institutions enhances professional gravitas and creates a win-win for both sides. The more prestigious the institution, the more powerful your own status can become—assuming it's a good fit. First and foremost, universities are looking for alignment with the institution's mission and values, your level of passion, and a genuine interest in education. Successful C-suite executives and board directors with experience in diverse sectors are highly sought after, though a C-level role is not always required.

Previous teaching experience or a history of volunteering in the educational sector is favored and can help you build visibility. Other ways to expand academic networks and get involved include teaching guest lectures or master classes, overseeing innovation labs, volunteering, or serving on boards. These entry points can often lead to part- or full-time opportunities that may evolve into longer-term roles. Outside of teaching, additional opportunities are also available in areas like administration and community engagement.

Teaching in academia is a powerful and enriching way to continue your learning, serve others, and build gravitas within your community. It frequently provides access to a more high-caliber network, which in turn can unlock other exciting synergies and new opportunities in business and beyond.

Boss-Minded Leaders Challenge the Status Quo by Asking Themselves:

▶ What areas of academia interest me: teaching or the administrative side?

▶ Do I already have contacts in academic institutions? Who could I reach out to learn more about their experiences and explore pathways to get involved?

▶ Am I willing to start with volunteering to network my way into a paid opportunity?

Own Your Brand:
The (Seemingly) Little Things

Back in Germany, there's a saying: *'Good manners will never go out of style.'* As you elevate your executive status, your public visibility will grow with you.

Therefore, personal refinement becomes increasingly important—not only for your career but also for navigating the polite society you'll encounter as you enter higher executive ranks, boardrooms, academic environments, and prestigious non-profit organizations.

In the following pages, we will explore the value of investing in your appearance and manners, how you speak, and better strategies for conducting yourself on social media—all of which will pay significant dividends. We'll also delve into the benefits of giving back and the often-overlooked art of entertaining as powerful tools for expanding your gravitas in new environments and at higher levels of society.

CHAPTER 20

Appearance—Look the Part, Win the Game

*"Elegance is not about being noticed, it's
about being remembered."*
—**Giorgio Armani**

Clients often protest when I point out that their appearance matters. They'll say things like, *"That's silly, everything's casual now! I recently saw the CEO of so-and-so on LinkedIn wearing sneakers and a shirt with no tie."* Then they tell me they'll stick with wearing worn-out sneakers, bulging slacks, and dated shirts because they don't have to impress anyone, and I don't know what I'm talking about. To prove a point, they sometimes text me a photo from said so-and-so.

Surprise often awaits, especially with men, when they read my response after looking at the photo they sent me: *"Actually, those sneakers are Italian and retail for $800 a pair. That's a $500 shirt, the same for the pants. Both have been custom tailored. The glasses are Versace, and the belt matches, adding another $1,000. The watch looks like a Breitling, so probably another*

$10-$15k at the low end, maybe more. You're looking at a minimum $15K casual outfit—and the guy didn't even bring his jacket."

At this point, jaws typically drop. A few weeks later, I usually receive a photo after a trip to Nordstrom or an upscale men's boutique, a fresh haircut, and a simple message: *"I get it now."* Voilà, congrats—it's a whole new you!

People don't always appreciate this fact, but image matters. Executives who hold power almost always look the part. Image encompasses both appearance and manners. The more high-value you appear, the more high-value you are perceived to be. If you want people to invest in you, it's advisable to look the part.

Powerful people wear quality clothing that's fitted and made from materials that maintain their shape and pristine look for years. The reason Daniel Craig looks so sharp on the red carpet is because he's wearing a custom-tailored suit, not a $500 polyester department store piece that was glued together in a Chinese sweatshop. If you see senior leaders in casual clothing or footwear, don't mistake it for cheap. Also, don't assume you can do the same—at least not until you're the next Mark Zuckerberg.

Yes, I'm fully aware that it's all rather superficial, but so is life. Here's the deal: life and careers are one big stage. Whether you want the audience to perceive you as the peasant or the king is up to you. Yes, performance should matter more than looks, and I'm not saying performance doesn't matter. What I'm saying is that your image—your brand, if you will—becomes increasingly important the higher up you go, because your visibility expands both internally and externally. The more visible you become, the more you need to step up your A-game. Not just because everyone around you is doing the same, but also because people will be paying attention. So, start leveling up.

What does this mean for you? Three things: First, learn the difference between short-lived fashion and timeless class. Second, understand the social codes of luxury items. Third, accept that quality comes at a price, and if you want to look the part, you'll likely need to spend some of your hard-earned money.

The advice is the same for both women and men: invest in quality pieces and tailoring if needed. Good tailoring not only improves fit but also enhances posture, boosting confidence. While women have more choices, timeless design tends to have a longer shelf life for both genders than fashion. Though some industries are more relaxed, the higher up you go, the more conservative the rules become—especially around quality clothing, elegant understatement in jewelry and accessories, and even subtle details like haircuts and beard styles. Most likely, 'hobo' isn't going to cut it anymore.

I often recommend hiring a professional stylist. Sometimes clients ask if their spouse can take on the task. No offense, but I'll say this: *"If they've let you leave the house looking like this for all these years without protest, you really may want to pay someone."*

The bottom line is that people will look at you differently when you dress the part—and this is truer today more than ever. Money spent on signature pieces that stand the test of time is a wise investment. If budget is a concern, there are many high-quality retail options for pre-owned luxury clothing, timepieces, and jewelry. Nobody will ever know. As Herbert Harold Vreeland once said, *"Clothes don't make a man, but clothes have got many a man a good job."*

With your appearance sorted, the next area to level up is the way you speak.

Boss-Minded Leaders Challenge the Status Quo by Asking Themselves:

▶ Am I looking 'the part,' even if I personally don't care much for superficialities?

▶ Am I dressed in a contemporary, elegant way, or do I still wear suits and hairstyles that are twenty years old?

▶ Do I understand the corporate and social codes of luxury?

▶ Would I feel more comfortable getting professional help with my shopping choices?

CHAPTER 21

Speak to Lead—Command Attention

"Be sincere, be brief, be seated."
—Franklin D. Roosevelt

This chapter is not about public speaking—though if that's an area for growth, definitely invest in it. Instead, it's about the basics of how to engage with senior executives who have everything: money, status, power…everything except time.

For this section, I reached out to the most impatient client I know—Jonathan. We collaborated well because my German approach of being straight to the point and working with efficient processes suited both his personality and his busy schedule. When I jokingly asked him what his impatience looks like in real life, Jonathan was… direct.

"If people can't get to the point, it's a red flag, and it's something you already see in interviews," he said. *"My personal hell is what I call 'RFP people.' Have you ever sat in an RFP where they start by talking about when and where the company was founded, then go on about how the business evolved, and finally get to the products*

they offer? I cut that right off after two minutes and tell them what I really want to know, so I can hand it over to my team and go talk to more important people."

Elaborating further on what he really wants to know in conversations, he added:

"In RFPs, most of the time, I only want to know three things: how and where they're different, the price, and how they'll go the extra mile for me as a customer. If I need to know about the other stuff, I'll ask. Don't make me sit through all this drivel. In presentations, my team knows that most of the time, I'm only interested in the last slide. In conversations, I want to know right away what you need from me, or what the issue, the proposed solution, or the desired outcome is.

It's not about speaking faster; it's about putting the relevant information at the front of the conversation, or you'll lose people."

Speaking with brevity and clarity is one of the greatest gifts you can offer a senior leader. In today's world of busy schedules and shortened attention spans, nobody has the time or capacity to listen to drawn-out monologues where the key point is buried deep in the story. In media, that is called 'burying the lede.'

Burying the lede is a major pet peeve for many. I once witnessed a CRO reprimand two of her Sales VPs in a staff meeting after an RFP went completely sideways. She wasn't normally one for public executions, but she deemed the waste of prospects' time so important that she turned it into a teachable moment for the team.

"If clients or bosses ask you a question, your job is to make the answer as short and clear as possible. Don't bury the lede by giving them a long-winded response and leaving it up to them to decipher what you mean. That's just poor customer service. Time is money, and when you're talking to someone who makes more money than you, their time is worth a lot more than yours. You need to treat that commodity with the utmost respect."

The biggest recommendation I give to executives—especially the rambling top-level ones who never receive the gift of being interrupted in their monologues—is to untrain themselves from the STAR method.

You're probably familiar with STAR: whether for interviewing or describing a past event, it advises you to first explain the situation, then the task, followed by the action you took, and finally the result. While the STAR method has its value, it's also a great way to put people to sleep. At the executive level, though, it's all about getting to the bottom line quickly. Similar to how Amazon builds all their processes backward from the targeted customer outcome, you want to start with the actual or desired results.

It's as simple as going to your boss and saying, *"Per my calculation we can save $1 million a year by changing technology providers."*

Now you have their attention—straight to the point. If they want to know the details, which they likely will because you've piqued their interest, they can ask. Or you can say, *"Want to know how I found this new company?"* Now you've shifted to a two-way conversation and turned the encounter into a consultative dialogue instead of a sleep-inducing monologue.

Versus: *"Remember after you approved the conference budget and I went to New York for that technology event last year where I spoke to this boutique company from Austin that does healthcare AI which is also where I used to live during college and then later again for my first job?"* (I know. I'm rolling my eyes with you. WHERE are we going with this?!) *"With how many problems we have on the automation side and the budget cut that's coming I was wondering if we maybe want to entertain the idea to switch providers because in looking at the numbers, we might be able to save some money... I'm estimating maybe low seven figures."*

My god. In my corporate days, I wanted to stab my eyes out with a fork listening to people like that. You can see the difference. If you want to kill your career, keep talking. If you want to get on a board, you might as well just bury that idea. There is no patience for that kind of nonsense in that world.

Here's a trick from my PR days when I trained executives for media: pause before you speak. Unless you want to intentionally ramble to kill time and deflect the question, take a moment to think before you say anything. Nobody will notice the pause. Ask yourself what the most important piece of information is that you want to convey, and then start with that.

Pay attention to people's reactions while you communicate. Are their eyes glazing over? Are they looking sideways or at their phones? If so, you're losing them. If you're losing them, you're boring—and that's the best-case scenario. The worst-case scenario is that they see you as a waste of space with an inflated sense of grandiosity, taking up valuable air time and unable to communicate concisely. *Not executive material.* Refined servant leaders speak less and listen more.

Improving your ability to speak concisely will make people look at you differently. It's not about being terse or short. The less you say and the more you can frontload important information, the more people will want to pay attention. Your executive presence will grow, and you'll drive efficiency, reducing confusion and misunderstandings. Of course, diplomacy, tact, and an empathetic delivery are still crucial, but they can be just as effective when we front-load our conversations with critical information.

After thousands of hours spent in largely unproductive meetings, I would argue that corporate life would be much more efficient and fun if more emphasis were placed on efficient delivery.

With polished manners, obviously.

Boss-Minded Leaders Challenge the Status Quo by Asking Themselves:

- ▶ Do I frequently lose people in meetings because I take up too much air time?

- ▶ Have I received feedback that I'm 'too chatty' or bury the lede?

- ▶ Have I asked for feedback on how my communication style is received? Should I? (Hint: If the idea of asking gives you a pit in your stomach, chances are you should.)

- ▶ For foreign executives: Have I received feedback that my accent is difficult to understand? Should I consider investing in accent reduction training?

CHAPTER 22

Manners—Confidence, Not Cringe

"Manners maketh man."
—**William of Wykeham**

A few years ago, a former leader of mine was hiring a Senior Director for our team. As is customary after a morning full of interviews, the candidate was taken to lunch. It's astonishing how many executives don't treat lunches and dinners as an integral part of the interview process. This is not the time to sit back and relax. It's a microscope situation, where people are watching closely: How does the candidate interact with the team? Do they engage with their peers and lower-ranking colleagues, or only with the higher-ups? How are their social skills in pleasantries and small talk? Are they courteous to the wait staff? Are they capable of eating with knife and fork and their mouth closed?

In this particular situation, the candidate went down forever as the 'Invisalign Guy.' Invisalign Guy famously extrapolated himself out of the hiring process through his savagely unrefined table manners.

Instead of excusing himself to discretely remove his retainers in the restroom, he pulled them out of his mouth at the table, rinsed them off in his water glass and then placed them on a napkin next to the mortified junior analyst. It was like watching a train wreck in slow motion. After the thorough retainer rinse, he pulled a toothbrush out of his coat pocket that looked like a dog's chew toy. That device was also neatly placed next to the cringing analyst so he *"won't forget to brush later."* Awesome.

It wasn't a surprise when the afternoon interview schedule was suddenly rearranged due to an urgent meeting with a C-level executive that unexpectedly popped up on my boss's calendar.

While the story might be hilarious, the sad part is that the candidate, despite having impeccable experience, likely never connected the dots and remained blissfully unaware that his poor etiquette cost him the job. Ignorance is dangerous. Blind spots will cost you.

Even when we have the fundamentals down, professional-grade manners and etiquette become harder to acquire as we age because our habits are already formed. A quick look around shows how much public manners have declined in recent years. The group of people willing to hold the door open for others is shrinking. Simple acts like saying 'please,' 'thank you,' and apologizing are being overlooked. Speaking loudly on speakerphones in public has become common. Many people seem to feel entitled to be inconsiderate to those around them. If you want to reach the upper echelons, you may need to stretch yourself a bit in the refinement and culture department.

Top executives in global companies, particularly those who find themselves on the international stage, often underestimate the rigorous expectations surrounding not just dress codes, but also etiquette and manners. Take someone like Carlos Ghosn, former CEO and Chairperson at Nissan. Before his career took an unexpected turn, he was one of the most powerful automotive CEOs in the world. Living the international jet-set life, he was frequently seen with political figures, other top-level leaders, and dignitaries worldwide. Ghosn was—and still is—supremely polished, exuding class and sophistication.

If you find yourself intimidated by formal dinners and networking events, consider investing in an etiquette class. It's a staple in international diplomacy training, and it should be for executives as well—especially for those with aspirations that will launch them into another stratosphere.

Even if you don't want to go that far, learning to sit up straight, keeping your elbows off the table, and using both knife and fork will elevate your status, confidence, and how others perceive you as a high-value person. At a minimum, it will help you impress a date or your spouse. At best, it'll put you at ease in future situations where you may be under the microscope or nervous about embarrassing yourself.

There's already plenty of opportunity for that in the virtual world.

Boss-Minded Leaders Challenge the Status Quo by Asking Themselves:

▶ Have I asked others how my manners are perceived, especially by higher-level people?

▶ Do I want to consider investing in this space, even if just for fun?

CHAPTER 23

Social Media—Less Noise, More Influence

"Nothing strengthens authority as
much as silence."
—Leonardo da Vinci

Thankfully it doesn't happen too often, but every once in a while, we have to have uncomfortable conversations and advise executive clients with C-level and board aspirations to scrub their social media. Anything that could be perceived as tacky, not adding value, divisive, upsetting to the customer base, or a risk to their personal brand needs to go.

Obviously, the individuals who fall into this category can sometimes be a little... I don't want to say combative, but let's call them 'passionate.' When I point out that it's in their best interest to delete a few things and limit access to their social media history, the pushback is often... impassioned.

"But, I'm a social justice activist; I feel like it's my duty and responsibility to use my voice to make a difference."

I applaud that—it's very honorable. And it truly breaks my heart when I have to say this, but if that's what they want, they should get a job at Greenpeace, PETA, or similar organizations. These are the perfect places for making an entire career out of being passionate.

Most leaders are well-advised to mirror the conduct of prominent CEOs and board directors. Their social media profiles are typically professionally monitored, with a curated strategy around thought leadership and dignified silence.

"But how can I be my authentic self then?" is often the follow-up question from those who haven't yet played the game at a high level. Here's another piece of uncomfortable news from a board director friend of mine: *"You don't get paid to be your authentic self. You get paid to do a job for the company — not to put the business in the firing line of public opinion with your personal beliefs or potentially divisive opinions."*

It's not always what people want to hear. People can do as they please, of course, but they should be aware that they're playing with fire.

While things are shifting slowly towards more relaxed public vulnerability and authenticity, there remains a very fine line. The needle for social media etiquette has barely moved at the top level in corporate communications and executive reputation management. It is still defined by privacy, scarcity, and a high level of scrutiny regarding where and when senior executives engage.

Here's another thing many top-level leaders don't do: they don't post pictures of their families and children. They maintain their privacy, both for safety reasons and because it helps them avoid looking common. The world runs on the principle of supply and demand, and superior status is maintained through scarcity.

After significant consumer backlash in 2023 and 2024 against companies like Budweiser (Bud Light), Target, Tractor Supply Company, and John Deere, many corporations have openly or quietly realigned their corporate messaging (and funding) to focus solely on matters that advance their business without alienating parts of their customer base.

Regardless of where we individually stand on topics like religion, politics, and social activism, the takeaway is clear: because these subjects are debatable matters of personal opinion—rather than objective facts like 'two plus two equals four'—there is significant value in keeping such beliefs private. Maintaining neutrality is a viable business strategy for both corporations and individuals. If people don't know what you think, they don't know what to attack.

I once had a client who became so wrapped up in a social justice issue that her highly searchable online persona gave her a reputation for being rigid, over the top, angry, and emotional—making her seem potentially difficult to work with. It not only ended her C-level career but also derailed her board director aspirations. The damning verdict from board recruiters was: 'Too excessive and combative for dignified public board service.'

This is just one example of how well-intended civic engagement can derail high aspirations. Meanwhile, others who maintain a lower profile skate through life and careers unscathed. Their reputation may carry a bit of mystery, but overall, people tend to conclude, 'They're easy to get along with and easy to work with.'

Your brand is what people say about you when you're not in the room. Therefore, choose wisely what you say on a public stage; you never know where your persona and conduct might be discussed and evaluated behind closed doors. If in doubt, it's advisable to stay focused on safe topics like thought leadership and industry insights. Silence is a virtue. Contrary to current societal trends, it is neither necessary nor in your best interests to voice your personal opinions at every opportunity.

How about focusing on activities that bring people together instead?

Boss-Minded Leaders Challenge the Status Quo by Asking Themselves:

▶ What impression could my social media give to an uninvolved outsider? Is there a chance I might be perceived as combative or divisive?

▶ What strategy do I want to follow? Do I want to be very visible and risk being perceived as common, or do I want to curate an elevated image of thought leadership and sophisticated scarcity?

▶ Should I consider scrubbing a few things or having my social media professionally managed?

CHAPTER 24

Entertaining—Strengthen Bonds, Expand Influence

"A guest never forgets the host who has treated him kindly."
—Homer

Thomas, a procurement executive, once shared his golden rule with me: he never lets a superior buy him a drink in a one-on-one setting unless it was for his birthday.

When I asked him why, he said, *"I never take for granted the fact that I owe my current opportunity to them. Yes, I work for them and at the end of the day, it's my job to make them look good, but I'm at their mercy. I always want to position myself from a place of gratitude."* With a wink, he added, *"Whether they deserve it or not."*

Psychologically, this makes sense due to the two tactics at play here: gratitude and the avoidance of entitlement, while also leveraging the reciprocity reflex. People almost always remember the good things others have done for them, even if they were small gestures. Picking up the tab may not guarantee the next promotion, but it builds goodwill, camaraderie, and triggers the reciprocity reflex. Quid pro quo. What comes around goes around, in business and in life.

While some may brand it as elitist and old school, hosting—as an ancient art form to build closer relationships—is more powerful than ever today. Creating intimate moments that matter goes a long way in a time where many people are glued to their phones all day but shy away from using it to call and stay in touch. How can you build business and relationships if you don't talk to people?

Few gestures are as powerful as breaking bread or sharing a drink together—whether it's after a game of golf, during a conference, at your home, while team-building, or as part of group getaways. In any situation where gratitude matters, which is almost anywhere, these moments create lasting bonds. It's how exclusive networks have been built and cultivated for thousands of years.

Giving back personally is another powerful way to build community and elevate your network.

Boss-Minded Leaders Challenge the Status Quo by Asking Themselves:

▶ In what easy ways could I stretch myself to curate experiences for others that foster a sense of camaraderie, unplugged quality time, and elevate relationships?

▶ If hosting at my home isn't possible or something I'm comfortable with, what other avenues could I explore to create moments that matter?

CHAPTER 25

Giving Back—The Slingshot Effect

*"If you light a lamp for someone else it will
also brighten your own path."*
—**Buddha**

A couple of personal stories.

An executive industry association once brought in the female CEO of an energy company for a speaking engagement. This was exciting because there still aren't many female CEOs in the energy sector. After the Q&A, I struck up a conversation and casually asked what she does to help younger women rise through the ranks in her field. She looked at me as if I had asked if she invented the lightbulb. *"I don't do any of that. In fact, I never do anything for anyone else,"* was her underwhelming response.

When I received my U.S. citizenship, the judge who administered my naturalization ceremony said something that has stayed with me: *"This country, this union we live in, isn't perfect. But it's the best we've got. How good it gets will largely depend on how much we, the people—and now you—help create a better society within our individual realm of influence."*

It's easy to get so wrapped up in our busy day-to-day lives that we neglect to create space for helping others and supporting the greater good through civic engagement. Aside from the benefits, such as a stronger sense of purpose, personal fulfillment, and more friendships, civic engagement becomes expected at a certain level in many societies, including the United States.

Within local non-profits, industry associations, executive groups, and professional organizations, there are plenty of opportunities to get involved—whether by giving money or time.

Due to the synergies that can be unleashed, it makes sense to invest in these opportunities. Engagement breeds visibility, and visibility breeds opportunity. Giving back and getting involved on boards and committees of high-profile non-profit organizations will expand your network and provide access to people you might not otherwise be able to connect with.

Often, senior executives are more willing to open doors for individuals they meet in informal environments than for people within their own organizations. Giving back and being a slingshot for others can not only create new professional opportunities but also open up entirely new avenues for speaking engagements, board service, academia, and advancing into the upper echelons of society.

Boss Tip:

Keep in mind that there is a hierarchy within the non-profit world. While your decision to support an organization should be driven by your passion for their cause, it's also true that connecting with high-profile leaders at the board or committee level offers a viable avenue for elevated networking. The more prestigious the organization, the higher the caliber of their board and committee members. This is a great opportunity to surround yourself with people who will push you to level up.

Boss-Minded Leaders Challenge the Status Quo by Asking Themselves:

▶ What is my personal brand and presence in the 'giving back' space?

▶ What areas might interest me for involvement? Should I stay focused on industry associations or explore broader charitable organizations?

▶ Do I have contacts in industry associations or non-profit organizations that I could leverage to create entry paths?

PART III

People Buy People

Your Personality
is Your Winning Edge

Unlock Your Best Self:
Developing Your Personality

Why does this book close with personality? Because your character will become a significant, if not *the*, deciding factor for how high your star will rise.

Like A Boss began with the disclaimer that the executive tactics and strategies to get more out of your working years don't work in a vacuum. Instead, they always dovetail into the dynamics of socio-economic ecosystems and the complexities of human interaction, group dynamics, and hierarchy structures.

In today's world, competencies can be compared apples-to-apples pretty easily. The vast majority of them are also not a commodity. At the end of the day, the differentiator for how far you will go will always be your personality, your friendliness, and whether you have authentic positive energy to draw others in.

All previous topics in this book have focused on optimizing your external knowledge of executive activity levers that drive additional ROI. Unless you're already a seasoned leader, your competencies have most likely been the key to climbing the ranks—both internally and externally—up to this point.

If anything ever breaks your future career, chances are it won't be your skills and expertise. Changing business conditions aside, roadblocks will most likely occur from unaddressed personality issues that may impact your ability to lead and influence successfully, unlock trust and goodwill, and gain access to high-caliber networks.

Relentlessly embracing a life of growth enables us to show up as the best version of ourselves at any given point in time, both for ourselves and others. As your star rises, you will need to increasingly influence politics through authentic positivity and friendliness. People will always buy people. The way you show up will become a key differentiator in whether you will get all the way to the top—or come close.

Let's look inwards.

CHAPTER 26

Blind Spots Will Cost You. Period.

"A man's character is his fate."
—Heraclitus

In today's world, where honesty is often a rare commodity, feedback is a gift. The story below illustrates how things can play out when we don't accept that gift and fail to take it seriously.

ABREO once served an outplacement client who I will only refer to as 'the candidate.' The candidate was among the top of their field. In fact, not just top of their field, but at a level where there was only a very small talent pool of people in the country who could do the job. The individual had an exceptional pedigree: Ivy League educated, tremendous experience, and checked a few other boxes that corporations tend to view favorably.

The reason for the termination quickly became clear. Despite all talents and professional accolades, certain behaviors were not suited for the organization's culture. In plain speak, the person had a reputation for being abrasive. Far from optimal and so blatantly obvious that even we, as an outside service provider who only get to see the tip of the iceberg, picked up on it immediately. For the individual, the behavior wasn't just a fit issue with the company that let them go, but a general problem.

While we would never ask where certain behaviors or beliefs stem from, sometimes it is possible to draw conclusions. This was a very sensitive situation because the individual blamed literally everything that happened to them on their specific minority status, taking it ad absurdum. Given the sensitivity, we will use a neutral hobby description—being a gardener—in place of their minority status.

The first thing the candidate told us was, *"I got fired because I'm a gardener."* Throughout the engagement, they also shared, *"My colleagues didn't like me because I'm a gardener. My boss didn't like me because I'm a gardener. My senior leadership team didn't like me because I'm a gardener. In the six months leading up to my termination, my stealth job search did not generate any results because gardening has been a 'structural barrier' for me in all of my conversations."*

Apparently, the country's entire elite recruiting community, including partners in top-level headhunting firms, disliked the candidate because they were anti gardening. Although, I'm not quite sure how anyone would have known about this particular minority status unless the candidate had disclosed it. This was not an ethnicity situation where their protected class was immediately obvious. In this case, things were a lot more subtle.

The victim thinking, blame-shifting, and lack of accountability for their behavior were plain to see for everyone—except the candidate. Allowing for space and pause, after a moment of reflection in one of our conversations, I heard something that made me think something was about to shift.

"You know, I think it's me," I heard, curious about where this would go.

"What are you thinking?"

"It's because I'm a gardener." The small flame of self-awareness had lost its glimmer of hope. *"Although someone recently gave me feedback that I was not friendly during an interview. They told me I never smiled and am terse,"* they continued.

"Oh yeah? What did you think about that?" I asked.

"Well yeah, that's bullshit obviously. We're not a fluffy industry; I reject that feedback. Even if my old company says that's why I got let go, deep down I know that wasn't the reason. It was because I'm a gardener and don't fit in. Whatever, it's fine. I've never fit in anywhere."

Interesting.

Getting hired for competence and fired for personality and attitude is alive and well, as seen from our gardening friend. Don't let that be you. You've worked too hard on your skills and experience to let hidden blind spots in your personality become your Achilles' heel and jeopardize your endgame.

Looking in the mirror takes courage. Ask yourself: What is my Achilles' heel? Nobody is perfect—we all have weaknesses. Impatience, false perceptions of how others see us, a short temper, blame-shifting, victim mentality, unfriendliness, arrogance, trust issues, or unchecked pride and ego can all hold us back from taking accountability or righting our wrongs. The possibilities for self-sabotaging our lives and careers are endless.

What is the one piece of feedback you've heard over and over again that you need to improve? Are you ready to accept it and do the work? Think about this seriously—because that one blind spot, the one thing you've resisted changing, could be the very obstacle that holds you back the most in business and life. There is a quote by Anaïs Nin that goes *"We do not see things as they are, we see them as we are."* **Who are you?**

With our unlucky horticulturalist, others saw the reality the candidate ignored—clear as day. It wasn't their minority status that turned people off; it was their unfriendliness, rooted in a deep-seated negative self-image. By projecting their inner negativity outward, they caused those around them to either retreat or retaliate, reinforcing the belief that being a minority candidate was the issue.

In truth, the real problem was how their internal struggles manifested externally, eroding goodwill and morale. **Blind spots will cost you.**

For the candidate, it was easier to continue their victim thinking than to look deep and change, so they continued on a path that ultimately got them fired. From my experience of working with clients in outplacement and my days in HR, I am not sure how many times some people need to hear the same feedback before they are willing to consider the idea that, despite their best efforts to feed the blame game narrative, the responsibility for their isolation usually tends to sit with *them*.

In the gardener's example, according to the CHRO, Albert, the history about their poor attitude was *"rather long to where they had heard it endless times in 360-reviews, and from suppliers, and clients."* This was in addition to recently being told by a well-meaning recruiter, apparently. Dismissing these revelations and failing to take them to heart became a direct hit to the candidate's career P&L.

Although growth is always possible, some people—despite overwhelming evidence—cling to their pride and insist that everyone else is wrong. Clients will sometimes say, *"I was told at work that I interrupt people too much, which is funny because my wife and kids say the exact same thing."* Soon, we'll uncover why resisting change is so common.

For now, how about this idea: if we repeatedly hear the same commentary from several people, what are the odds that there might be some truth to it? Here's another thought-provoking idea: if everyone around us is wrong, does that mean we have a habit of surrounding ourselves with—pardon the bluntness—stupid people? After all, according to that logic, we're the only ones who are ever right, right?

This is where clients will always protest and say, *"Of course not, how dare you! My wife/husband isn't stupid!"* My response is always, *"Well, then what alternative does that leave us with?"*

I rest my case. Entire companies have gone bankrupt because people were too focused on being right. The real question is: *do you want to be right, or do you want to reach your goals?*

Boss-Minded Leaders Challenge the Status Quo by Asking Themselves:

▶ What feedback have I received repeatedly about areas of my personality or approach with others that I should change?

▶ Why have I repeatedly dismissed this feedback in the past?

- Have I been too focused on being right? Is it time to embrace humility and acknowledge where I might have been wrong, treated others poorly, or was arrogant?

- Could I be the source of my problems since they seem to repeat themselves?

CHAPTER 27

Win By Choice—Not By Chance

*"Good words are worth
much and cost little."*
—George Herbert

Positive energy and personality naturally generate goodwill. In business, an engaging and authentically pleasant character is essential for navigating the tactical and diplomatic demands of upper-echelon corporate careers.

Hard work, skills and competencies, or knowing every trick in the book of negotiation and self-advocacy will only get people so far. The higher we go, the more it's no longer just about getting the job done. It's now about strategic leadership, exerting influence, and building trust, alliances and partnerships to drive change and rapid progress. With a magnetic personality, achieving these goals will be much easier than if others can't stand us.

Another angle to drive this home is, it's not what you know, it's who you know. In the end, you will get ahead not only based on your performance but also by the relationships you cultivate. Without a positive, curious, and winning demeanor (something that has to authentically come from the inside or it will always be perceived as fake and untrustworthy), building alliances with the right people will become a significant challenge.

Good salespeople have always understood that friendliness and great personalities sell. If you think about it, in the end, everything we do in life is essentially sales. Friendliness, attitude, and positive energy play the same vital role in the corporate world.

Throughout my career, I've seen time and again that well-liked individuals are often promoted—even if they lag slightly in competency. They receive a trust advance, with the assumption that they'll figure things out with the support of their teams once they step into the role. Especially when, per Gallup's data, two-thirds of people are disengaged (and therefore often not a joy to be around), authentic positivity is powerful. All this makes personality development a high ROI area worthy of your long-term investment.

With the example of our unhappy gardener, the company was right not to tolerate a toxic leader, frustrated suppliers, and low morale any longer. Concerns like these are rarely surface level issues. In order for change to be sustainable, the work has to go deeper.

Albert, the CHRO who trusted ABREO with the gardener exit summarized it well: *"Nobody will become a friendlier person because their 360-review tells them they are rude and have a negative attitude. Sure, they may be able to course-correct a little, but if the overall inner attitude isn't there, there really is no solid foundation that will make them an optimistic and friendlier person in the general sense. The entire construct will fall apart like a house of cards. Sometimes it's just easier to cut ties and hope that events like these will serve as a wakeup call. Maybe they will do some inner work and take control of their happiness so it can transcend outwards. Just not with us, we're out of gas, out of patience, and out of time."*

It's understandable that the time required for inner work and course correction exceeded the corporation's patience. With the wisdom of his later years, Albert knew that *a person's attitude always precedes and defines their behavior.*

While in this situation the outer career impact of a misaligned attitude was obvious, it was the deeper inner truth that made this case so sad. Everything that happened in the candidate's outer world was a mirror of the negative world view and self-image playing out internally. Naturally, if we don't like who we see in the mirror, we'll struggle to like ourselves and be genuinely friendly towards others as well.

The most important relationship we have in life will always be the one we have with ourselves. With that in mind I would argue that self-development is a worthwhile pursuit and an inside job that should continue as long as we live.

Healing and growth often don't occur in isolation but in community. Surrounding ourselves with people who are invested in our growth, whether it is certain leaders, therapists, coaches, friends, partners, mentors, or accountability buddies will force our hand and help us level up. Leveling up is the best way to show up—for ourselves, for others, and for the rising standards expected of us at the next level in business and life.

You probably know people like the gardener—those who tend to drain energy. Then, there are those who radiate positivity and effortlessly draw people in. So, who would you rather work with? Who would you trust and follow in times of uncertainty and change? Who would you choose to hire or promote? *Who would you rather be?*

Change is always possible but it's a choice. When real, sustainable growth happens, it doesn't just transform your career—it impacts your life as a whole.

Boss-Minded Leaders Challenge the Status Quo by Asking Themselves:

▶ Given what I've been hearing about myself and what I want to change, would it make sense to find an accountability buddy, coach, or mentor to help me grow into the next version of myself?

▶ Which connections and relationships have I outgrown that no longer meet my standards or hold me back?

▶ Who can I surround myself with instead to help elevate my growth?

CHAPTER 28

Change Happens When You Do

"The first step towards getting somewhere
is to decide you're
not going to stay where you are."
—JP Morgan

Our CHROs report that they frequently invest significant sums in rehabilitative executive coaching—only to end up terminating the leader anyway.

"Sometimes, internal relationships have deteriorated beyond repair, making it too late to turn the ship around. Other times, pressing business needs demand immediate action. More often than not, corporations simply don't have the time to wait for the lengthy transformation of complex personal attitude issues that undermine performance and stakeholder relationships."

Dennis, VP HR

Critics of the billion-dollar coaching industry will sometimes flippantly say that the secret behind its growing market share in recent years lies in the fact that coaching doesn't work. They argue the chase for growth makes this space a lucrative, never-ending cash cow because of how difficult it is to actually achieve sustainable change. Think as you wish, of course, but most of us can probably relate to one undeniable truth: meaningful change is hard.

Personal transformations are challenging because they often clash with our survival-based legacy thinking, leading to resistance. From an evolutionary perspective, change is threatening to the brain because we risk survival if the new approach doesn't succeed.

Sound familiar? That's because while no two brains are the same, our evolutionary wiring (and thinking) is something we all share: *"I've survived this far with how I act and think. Who knows if a different approach to fight the lion will work. I think I'll stick with what has always kept me safe and made me successful so far."* Or: *"Everyone else is wrong, I'm right."*

Marshall Goldsmith, a legend in the executive coaching space, puts it succinctly in his book, *What Got You Here Won't Get You There.* He explains that the habits and personality traits that got us to where we are today are unlikely to be sufficient for reaching or succeeding at the next level.[9.] In his widely acclaimed work, which is considered the gold standard of American executive coaching, Goldsmith highlights twenty common habits that can hold people back from reaching the top—and offers strategies for course correction.

While I reference Goldsmith's work often with clients who want to tweak certain behaviors, in my opinion, for many people it doesn't always go deep enough. If we look at bad habit #8, Negativity, for example, Goldsmith's recommendation—at least in the book—stops at observing speech patterns to detect negativity. It's solid advice, because awareness is a crucial first step.

However, as many of us know from past attempts at self-improvement, trying to contain unfavorable traits at the behavioral level simply through awareness, rationality, and willpower will be difficult and likely not lead to results that last.

For example, individuals like our gardener who exhibit massive negativity at work often carry that same energy into their personal lives. I've never met a pessimistic, low-energy, whiny, or cynical executive at work who was the life of the party after hours. Have you?

The difference between an executive with a "Negative Nancy" reputation and their more open, optimistic, and positive peer isn't just in their behavior. Behavior is surface-level. It's not even solely in the way they think—thinking is still fairly close to the surface.

It's their underlying mood and attitudes that truly set them apart. My observation aligns with Albert's assessment: our inner mood precedes our thoughts and behaviors. So, if we want to change anything, we need to start at the deeper level of attitude.

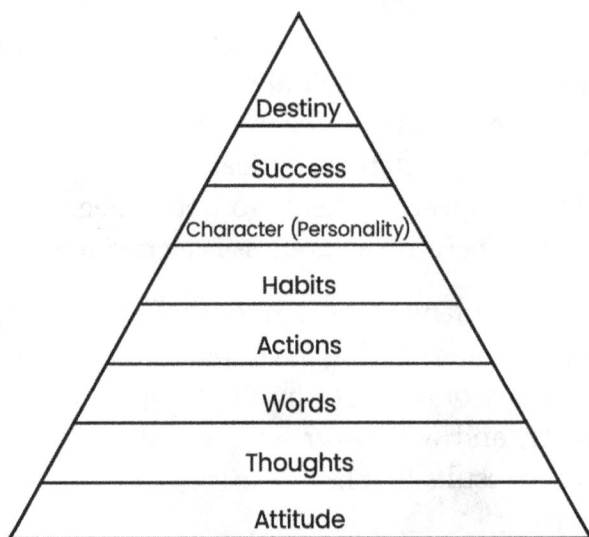

There is a famous quote from Lao Tzu, *"Watch your thoughts, they become your words; watch your words, they become your actions; watch your actions, they become your habits; watch your habits, they become your character; watch your character, it becomes your destiny."*

I believe Tzu's quote is ready for an update, beginning with: ***"Watch your attitude because it becomes the foundation for your thoughts, and so forth."***

The monumental challenge we face in improving our personalities is that it's difficult to do solely through willpower, even when we recognize it might be good for us.

In other words, deciding to be friendlier—or changing other behaviors for career benefits—will be difficult if we don't first adjust our attitude to genuinely feel more optimistic about life. As poet Walter D. Wintle wisely said, *"You can't win in the outer world if you're losing in your mind."*

Many wildly successful upper management executives and board directors I spoke with shared that their ability to shift and control their underlying mood and attitude became the foundation of their winning character. This ability, in turn, became the most important contributor to their success, as their magnetic personalities helped open doors in both business and life.

If we want to grow and improve our personality, the question isn't just about changing our behavior. The *real* million-dollar question is: **How can we shift our attitude to foster a more positive mood about life itself so the behavior can follow?**

Boss-Minded Leaders Challenge the Status Quo by Asking Themselves:

▶ How do I perceive the human experience overall—positively or negatively?

▶ Could my mood and attitude about life be affecting my behavior, relationships and career in a negative way?

CHAPTER 29

Attitude Adjustment—The Key to Unlocking Success

"We are all in the gutter, but some of us are looking at the stars."
—Oscar Wilde

As mentioned in the introduction, radical top performers have a unique ability to joyfully embrace and navigate life's endless ups and downs (Panta Rei).

I once had a fascinating conversation about this topic at a bar in Chicago. Sitting next to me was Cindy, a seasoned no-nonsense HR executive at a major consumer staples company. She had launched her career in people management fifteen years earlier after earning a master's degree in Psychology. Over a couple of drinks (or maybe a few more), we pondered how some people manage to skate through life with a brighter mood, better attitudes, and more endearing personalities than others.

Throughout the conversation, Cindy explained the (attitude) — (behavior/personality) — (success) triangle in simple terms. She began by clarifying that our personality is shaped by how we feel, think, and act (commonly known as our behavior).

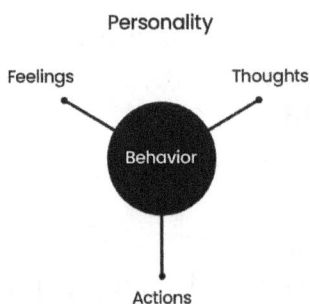

Personality

Feelings   Thoughts

Behavior

Actions

Attitude-Personality-Success Triangle

Success

Attitude   Personality/Behavior

"People who are consistently negative often struggle more with life's downsides than those who accept that, every once in a while, the shit will hit the fan. Those who resist the natural ebb and flow of life, believing it should always be smooth, are typically more prone to negativity and unfavorable behaviors. This doesn't just show up when things don't go their way, but in their overall demeanor. These individuals often complain, remain in a perpetual bad mood, have anger issues, and are arrogant or rude—behaviors that ultimately hinder their progress. People

don't want to work with them because they lack the maturity to handle challenges and life with grace. As adults, we should recognize that rainy days are part of life. Resisting that reality with permanent negativity doesn't solve anything—it only makes life <u>more</u> difficult."

Thinking of all the people I know who throw hissy fits over the small stuff—*'I'm dealing with a real crisis here!' Really? Because the cafeteria ran out of creamer??'*—I couldn't help but chuckle. It just felt so basic.

Playing devil's advocate, I pushed back. I suggested that expecting people to embrace things like a flat tire, losing their job or a loved one, or dealing with a difficult boss with relentless positivity—and without an emotional reaction—might be asking a bit much.

Cindy clarified that it's not that emotions like fear, grief, anger, sadness, disappointment, and so forth don't have their place. They are primary components of our emotional regulatory system, just like joy and other positive feelings. These emotions need to be expressed so we can process our new reality and move on. It's okay to be periodically sad, angry, or disappointed. The problem arises when we perpetually stay in that state, as it tends to become unhealthy for us.

I said I understood what she meant but not how people could change. In that moment, I was also reflecting on myself. My own blind spots crossed my mind, particularly how my attitude about certain areas of life used to subconsciously shape the way I showed up in the world and how they had impacted my personal and professional P&Ls. While Cindy didn't use the words Panta Rei specifically, this concept was essentially what her next explanation boiled down to.

"Life marches to the beat of its own drum, and sometimes it plays in tune with our instrument, and sometimes it doesn't. That's just life. Arrogance, throwing tantrums, being negative, etc., are 'childish reactions.' When you're a toddler and you spill your milk, you scream, and Mom comes to clean it up. But as an adult, you don't scream. You react quickly, clean it up, and pour yourself a new glass. Screaming, sulking, or complaining for prolonged periods of time doesn't change the reality—adapting does. Spilling milk is part of life, just like dealing with an employee who doesn't deliver, rain that disrupts your plans, or an Amazon parcel that doesn't show up on time. None of these things should make you a bitter person with a negative outlook on life."

I understood that—but it's easier said than done. As I reflected on the things that used to make me lose my temper, I asked Cindy how attitude, personality, and behavior fit together.

"It's pretty simple," she said. *"Psychologically and philosophically, everything starts with our attitude—how we feel and think about life. If we want to develop our personality (the mix of our feelings, thoughts, and actions) to become more positive and optimistic, we need to first retrain our brains to view life positively rather than maintaining a negative outlook."*

"But what about the flat tire and the annoying boss?" I asked. "Are you seriously saying that we shouldn't just accept but actually be _happy_ about the downsides of life?"

"It's not about being happy when things go sideways or not getting upset," Cindy said. "We'll still get frustrated. The fact that we got sick even after getting a flu shot, the stock market going down, or the neighbor running over our cat—these things _are_ unsettling. The difference in people with a better attitude is that they fundamentally understand that these events are the price we pay for still having the privilege to get up in the morning and participate in life on this little planet."

"And that will give me a more charming personality? The fact that I embrace my neighbor running over the cat as just part of life??"

We both laughed and ordered another round.

"Essentially yes," Cindy answered. "Because while you will naturally experience grief, which is the expected human reaction, you will also understand that 'these things happen.' If you get a pet, it could die. If you take a job with someone else, you could lose it. If you go skiing, you could break a leg. That's the risk you take by showing up. It's your admission fee for being part of the party, versus staying home or being dead. The difference is you won't stay in those emotional states forever. You'll process them and move on."

I thought the idea of treating life's shit-happens moments—or unfavorable outcomes as Cindy put it—as our admission fee was interesting. Cindy continued:

"Life and its events aren't inherently good, mean, or bad. Life isn't out to get you. Life is just... life. Periodically, things will happen that don't align with our wishes or objectives. These are opportunities to learn and adapt. When you master the ability to view life's downsides as your admission fee, because they will happen whether you fight them or not, you can approach the human experience with less hostility. That's when the real shift happens. When you can view life in a friendlier way, the world will feel less scary and more welcoming. You will become friendlier because you'll feel safer. You will realize that just being <u>against</u> the world and what's happening in your life <u>won't change anything.</u> This is when you can not only find solutions, like cleaning up spilled milk, but also pour yourself a new glass. A friendlier inner attitude toward life cures many issues — not just negativity, but also arrogance, impatience, and a lot of other issues."

To me, it sounded like personality development and how we feel, think, and act was more about training our brain to see life's obstacles with greater acceptance. The idea was that by *feeling safer*, we naturally become friendlier toward life and those around us. It made me think of Albert again, who had also said that attitude precedes our behavior and, later, our destiny. I shared what he said with Cindy.

"Absolutely," she said. *"Changing your attitude and becoming more friendly toward life — both its good and bad parts — will make you more friendly toward the world and the people in it. You will be more grateful for everything you already are and have versus always being focused on what's missing. As a result, you'll be received positively, which will*

pave the way for your success. People generally gravitate toward friendly folks with good energy."

Given the Gallup disengagement numbers, I often wonder how they might shift if more people were able to change their attitudes about their careers by first thinking differently about life in general.

In my decade-long collaboration with extraordinary leaders, I noticed a common trait among the most successful ones. These leaders radiate authentic positive energy that naturally draws people in. They don't just survive—they *thrive*, even when things don't go as planned. What sets them apart is their remarkable ability to stay calm and optimistic, even in the most stressful situations. While many people see setbacks and negative changes as obstacles, these leaders view them as opportunities. It's as if their ability to embrace life's downsides without succumbing to despair or excessive complaining has not only *illuminated their personalities* but also paved the way for their *great success.*

When I asked these leaders how they achieved this inner attitude, they often said the secret lies in approaching the human experience as a never-ending learning opportunity. Sounds easier said than done, right? That's because, before you can courageously step through the door of learning to try new things and grow, you first have to get past the guard.

The guard's name is fear.

Say hello to fear.

Boss-Minded Leaders Challenge the Status Quo by Asking Themselves:

▶ Would it be worthwhile to explore personality development techniques that could help me become a more optimistic and positive person, enabling me to harness greater positive energy in both my work and personal interactions?

▶ Who could assist in this process?

CHAPTER 30

Fear is Your Door to More—From Wanting to Doing

"The greatest mistake you can make
in life is to be continually
fearing you will make one."
—Elbert Hubbard

Whether you'll get your money's worth from this book will depend greatly on your ability to overcome your fears and summon the courage to start applying what you've learned. Gaining knowledge from a book is one thing; taking action and doing more is an entirely different story.

I often encounter leaders with immense talent, capabilities, and strong personalities who are paralyzed by the fear to fail, change, and take things to the next level. Many seasoned and accomplished leaders I speak with admit, *"I know I need to change or take action. The reason I'm holding back isn't because I think I'm right or because I'm lazy. I'm not starting because I'm afraid. Which sounds so stupid."*

It's not stupid. It's completely understandable. Fear is the biggest barrier between wanting to change and actually doing it. As you already know, from an evolutionary standpoint, our brain is wired to resist change. Change is perceived as a threat to our survival if the new method doesn't work. Our brain tells us to stick with what always worked.

The good news is that overcoming fear is a muscle that can be strengthened. It starts by recognizing that fear is simply our brain and nervous system's way of protecting us, alerting us to danger through the familiar physical symptoms. While our brain and nervous system mean well, they don't get to run the show, and we don't have to let them. Not every challenge we face is a life-or-death situation like encountering a lion in the caveman days, even if our survival-wired brain tries to convince us otherwise. Ultimately, we control how and what we think.

If we don't push past our fears and take risks, we won't experience growth, expand into new territories, or develop new skills and behaviors. So, how can we overcome our survival-based brain wiring and fears, moving from wanting to change to *actually changing*? How do we shift from wanting more to doing more?

Over the years, I've heard many courageous leaders say, *"Fear is my door to more."* When we dare to step past that guard, *more* can enter our lives—more knowledge, opportunities, relationships, fun, love, money, you name it.

We get braver simply by doing, because that's how the brain learns. It's showing up to that networking event, even though the thought of not knowing anyone terrifies us. It's getting that NACD credential, even though textbook learning scares us because we were never a great student. It's taking accountability for our behavior, apologizing, and righting our wrongs to repair important relationships in our lives. It's stepping up and giving that speech or presentation with sweaty palms and a beating heart. It's daring to negotiate that job offer despite our deeprooted fear of rejection. As they say, 90 percent of life is showing up.

Overcoming what scares us by actually *doing it* creates new connections in our brain and a newfound sense of safety. We all know that incredible feeling when we push past fear and accomplish something new: *"Phew, this negotiation wasn't as scary as I thought! All I had to do was say that I didn't think we were quite there yet, and they threw in a sign-on bonus and another week of vacation.*

I can't believe how easy that was! I'm so proud and happy! Next time, I'll ask for the conference budget and business class travel too!" Boss move—this is how it's done!

If we dare and do more, more can enter our lives. At its core, what happens here is simple learning. By overcoming our fears of something new, we learn something new. Through learning and practice, things get easier, we grow more confident, and fear starts to retreat. Just starting sounds so easy, but fear is a powerful guard at the door to more. So, the first question is not how do we overcome fear, but **how do we make it easier for ourselves to learn?**

Before we answer that, let's pause for a moment. Have you ever tried to learn something new during a major stress period in your life, such as during a divorce, job loss, financial struggles, or grief? If you have, you probably remember how difficult, if not impossible, it was. Our brain literally struggles to learn when we're stuck in survival mode. And why is that? **Because survival mode equals fear.**

For instance, it's well understood today that children who grow up in homes with physical or psychological abuse often struggle with poor academic performance. Fear stifles the brain, limiting both creativity and learning.

We also know that our brains and nervous systems can't distinguish between real threats to our safety and imagined ones. On a danger scale, the work crisis we're facing is objectively nothing like a lion trying to eat us. But it can feel that way. When it does, our ability to take action becomes limited. With rising rates of mental health conditions and anxiety prescriptions, many of us seem to operate in a constant state of survival mode—overwhelmed by the relentless pressures, challenges, conflicting responsibilities, and time constraints of our personal and professional lives.

Survival mode means fear. And fear means we can't learn or innovate. When the real or imagined lion in front of us is threatening to eat us, we don't pause and think, *What new tools can I add to my toolbox to handle this situation more innovatively, efficiently, and successfully?* No. Fight or flight kicks in. You either grab the weapon from your tool belt that you know how to use best and beat the shit out of the lion, or you run. Those are your options. As you've probably experienced, there's not much room for personal development in moments of crisis; real or imagined.

Bottom line: We cannot learn when our brain is in a state of fear and stress. If we can't learn, we can't grow. And if we can't grow, we can't change. Without change, we can't become more successful.

So, back to the question: how can we overcome our fears and make it easier to learn, so we can grow and change our personality and then our outward behavior?? How can we find the courage to walk past the guard of fear and step through the door of learning?

The answer is: **By making learning feel safe.**

Boss-Minded Leaders Challenge the Status Quo by Asking Themselves:

▶ What are my biggest fears in life?

▶ How much have these fears and past behaviors already 'cost me'?

▶ Where in my life have I paid the price for instinctively approaching situations like conflict, change, or disappointment, instead of walking through the door of learning towards change?

▶ What 'more' lies within reach behind my personal door?

CHAPTER 31

The Success Formula—Purpose, Learning, & Growth

> *"The mystery of human existence lies not just in staying alive, but in finding something to live for."*
> —Fyodor Dostoyevsky

Frank, a global technology executive and fellow German, had received support from ABREO after a difficult exit. During his fifteen-month gap between jobs, he took time to focus on his mental health, spending some of that time in a clinic to *"get himself straightened out"* after years of battling depression and high-functioning alcohol abuse.

When a college friend got married and the bachelor party brought him to Nashville, he invited me out to thank me for our support in finding his next opportunity. Over dinner, he shared his experience with me. I was happy to see him in much better shape than he had been months earlier when we worked through his exit.

"You know," he said as he opened up, *"there were obviously many factors that contributed to losing my job, like my addiction, for example. During my recovery, I came to realize that the one thing that caused me the most pain in the last few years of my life was that I didn't really understand why I was doing what I was doing or why I was even here. The money was nice, but it wasn't enough. I wasn't fulfilled, and I struggled with the question of what my purpose was. Not having that answer—and never finding it—only deepened my depression and fueled my downward spiral of hopelessness and drinking. It became a vicious cycle that only got worse."*

Seeing that he was doing better, I asked how he had solved this conundrum—especially since no one seems to have a definitive answer to life's purpose. He smiled, raised his glass, and said, *"By making it up!!"*

What does the topic of purpose have to do with making learning safer, improving your personality, moving from wanting to doing, and reaching higher levels of success? Depending on your mindset, it could be a roundabout way—or it could be a shortcut.

Let's keep an open mind and unpack this.

We should never be afraid to take charge and think for ourselves—both in business and in life—beginning with asking the hard questions.

When you ask Google "What is my purpose in life?" it returns 934,000,000 search results. It seems like Frank wasn't the only one looking for an answer that doesn't formally exist.

Having a sense of purpose is known to provide direction and serve as a driving force in life. Biologically, our primary purpose seems to be to survive long enough to procreate; everything else is *extra*. Beyond that, the lines tend to get a little blurry. Religions, societies, and institutions all work very hard to sell us their version of what we should believe, based on their doctrines. But the truth remains—if they're honest—no one really knows *for sure* why life exists or why we are here.

Maybe Frank was onto something and finding our purpose really is an inside job? It seems reasonable. Philosophically, religiously, and socially, people hold different beliefs about purpose. That makes sense. It is obviously a very personal spiritual question considering that nobody seems to have come up with the official 'real' answer yet. Until someone officially cracks the code, maybe we can take some pressure off by leveraging Frank's approach? Sort of as a *placeholder* until the 'real deal' answer comes around?

(If you're already content with your personal sense of purpose, that's wonderful, and this may not be for you.

Maybe your purpose is being a great parent, a mentor, or a philanthropist. Perhaps your career is your purpose, or maybe it's simply to live your best life. Whatever it is, do you.)

I applauded Frank for his independent thinking. Given that he's also German, I shouldn't have been surprised. German thinking has long been profoundly influenced by the humanist and philosopher Immanuel Kant. At the heart of his philosophy is the concept of intellectual enlightenment. In simplified terms, and within the context of his time (he lived from 1724 to 1804), Kant introduced the rebellious idea that people should think for themselves, rather than subjugating their thoughts to the interpretative sovereignty of institutions like—back then—the Church and State. Instead, he argued, they should rely on their own reason and rationality.[10]

Kant would be proud of Frank. Choosing independent thought over mindless crowd-following is a concept that hasn't aged—and is more relevant than ever as we carve out answers for our purpose and, as in Frank's case, greater happiness in life.

Of course, I had to ask him how he defines his purpose now. His answer was surprisingly simple: *"My purpose, from what I can tell, is that I am here to grow and learn to navigate life's challenges without despair. That's it. That's my purpose in business and in life—until someone qualified on the matter convinces me otherwise."*

Considering that life is fundamentally about never-ending growth (whether we like all the parts that come with it or not), the idea of adapting learning as a purpose placeholder is both a simple and genius life hack. Learning to navigate Panta Rei—the continuous flow of peaks and valleys, where everything changes and nothing stays the same—seems to be the common denominator of our collective human experience. Regardless of any and all other reasons for being here, it seems that, *fundamentally*, all of us are here to learn. **What could be the benefits of adopting learning as our purpose?**

I reached out to top management and board-level connections, asking if they'd be willing to be vulnerable with me. From the responses I gathered, it became clear that many senior executives have already adopted the 'learning as purpose' concept. They reported it has positively shaped their personalities and helped keep fear-based reactions in check.

Here is the summary of what powerful leaders said about the benefits of the learning-personality-success connection:

Leader One:

"My learning mindset makes me feel safer about stepping past the guard of fear and toward greater growth. With learning as my purpose, I can view the world, including my life and career, as one big playground where every experience is simply a new lesson to master.

With that attitude, failure and change became less intimidating. When learning is your life's and career's mission, failure becomes part of the equation—it's expected when you're working to get better at something new.

Without fear, I learn more effectively. I think more innovatively, and I move from wanting to doing more quickly because life and careers become one big, fail-safe learning playground. While others stagnate in front of their guard, you're making progress by acquiring new skills and real experiences. If you're no longer afraid of failure or setbacks, your brain feels safer, and that safety becomes the foundation for your personality and making moves."

Leader Two:

"Viewing the world with a mindset of lifelong learning and pairing that with an acceptance of life's downsides enables me to have a friendly outlook towards life, people, and the constant change that surrounds us. It lowers my inner resistance to the inevitable low points and ever-changing circumstances.

I understand that valleys are part of life, and eventually, the pendulum will swing the other way again. I've accepted this as a fundamental law of life, and my job as a lifelong learner and leader is to navigate these ups and downs with a positive attitude to make things easier—not just for myself, but for others as well."

Whether you adopt a learning mindset as a general approach to life or embrace it as your purpose isn't what matters most. The purpose-placeholder concept is simply a philosophical shortcut for those who struggle with the absence of a formal answer to life's biggest question.

For high-profile leaders, the *real magic* happens when they accept the law of life's ups and downs and *pair it* with the learning mindset to make learning safer. Not just to accumulate knowledge, although that's naturally the first step and a foundation for achievement. But more so because of how that safety positively impacts their personality and drives their success.

Leader Three:

"When I learned to stop fearing and resisting the peaks and valleys, I was able to embrace life in all its facets, experiences, and lessons. Paired with my learning mindset, I can now view life as a friendlier place. Not just life, but everything in it—people, circumstances, change. Nothing is inherently good or bad; it just is—lessons to be learned on my journey.

This friendly outlook, I suppose, is what sets my personality apart because I no longer operate from a scarcity mindset or place of fear. Some call it a 'magnetic personality.' Once I reached the upper levels of management, it was that general inner mood and elevated attitude that helped me navigate challenging situations without falling into blatant negativity and resistance. It allowed me to build more relationships and connections, opening even more doors, and really accelerated my success in every area of life.

My recommendation is simple: watch your mood and attitude about life. They are the fundamental underlying factors that determine how you show up in the world and, ultimately, shape your destiny."

While I chose negativity as an example, there are many overt and covert behaviors that can sabotage our lives and careers. With expert guidance, all of them can be traced back to how we fundamentally view the human experience itself—as either a positive or negative space. Seasoned leaders know that everything starts with their overall attitude toward life, and they don't shy away from digging deep. It's a fundamental part of choosing growth and ruling yourself first. There is wise quote from Buddha that says, *"Before you set out to conquer the world, first conquer yourself."*

Summary:

1. Learn to embrace Panta Rei as a fundamental law of life to control your underlying *attitude* about the human experience. Subsequently, your *overall* personality and behavior will expand favorably.

2. Pair Panta Rei with a learning mindset or purpose to make learning feel *safer*.

3. With learning getting safer and easier, step past the guard of fear through the *door to more*. Open your world to more opportunities in business and in life.

Your chosen purpose, inner mindset about your career and life, and approach to personality development as the foundation for your behavior will be deciding factors for the size of your kingdom.

Ultimately, the choice of what kind of king you will become is *yours*.

Boss-Minded Leaders Challenge the Status Quo by Asking Themselves:

▶ Do I struggle with finding purpose, and is this an area I'd like to explore further?

▶ Do I want to embrace learning as a 'fail-safe' purpose placeholder, or at least apply it as a key concept to reduce the pressure in my life and career?

▶ How comfortable am I with the concept of Panta Rei and evanescence? Does the idea that everything changes and nothing stays the same scare me, or does it empower me to navigate uncertainty with a learning mindset, comfort, and joy?

▶ Would it be worthwhile to engage a professional to help me explore these areas more deeply?

My Story: The Road to Here

"Not knowing when the dawn will come
I open every door."
—Emily Dickinson

People love making assumptions. I often hear: *"How is it possible that so many senior leaders need help navigating their careers and transitions? Most of your clients have spent many years in corporate—shouldn't they know how the world works by now?"*

Well. It's very obvious that clearly not everyone *just knows.* It doesn't work like that.

First, unless leaders grew up with highly educated parents in high-profile positions at large companies, the knowledge needed to navigate the cutthroat realities of corporate life isn't something casually passed down at the family dinner table.

Second, unless people grew up with wealth, they don't typically have the connections or refined manners needed to break into and navigate certain circles with ease. Success always comes more easily from an elevated starting position—one that includes education and access.

America is—and likely always will be—a land of opportunity for those willing to grind it out and overcome their pasts. That's what makes this country such an incredible place to live in. The theme of overcoming is a shared experience among corporate C-suite executives. Our clients are no exception.

Many of our leaders didn't come from wealth or an elevated social starting position. Many were the first in their family to attend college, earn an advanced degree, or break through the ranks of middle management. Others have risen above unthinkable personal circumstances or rebounded from career setbacks that would have been insurmountable for most.

Others are first- or second-generation immigrants whose families started with nothing. Anyone with that kind of history has to learn everything from scratch, and then once over in a new socio-economic environment that may present unique challenges and systemic restrictions. Succeeding in a foreign country often means overcompensating with an incessant work ethic, and a lot of trial and error.

That is my story as well.

The attributes that defined my path the most have always been relentless discipline, overcoming fear, risk-taking, personality traits that made working with clients easy and fun, and a commitment to continuous learning. Especially learning to deal with failure, a lot.

I earned two advanced degrees and graduated at the top of my class—after first failing in Agricultural Engineering. After two years of hard vocational farm training, that was a little unfortunate. Despite my eventual academic success, I later abandoned my PhD. My corporate career also included some spectacular professional failures. While these experiences were not particularly fun at the time, none of them turned into big personal, professional, or financial setbacks. In fact, quite the opposite actually.

Overcoming my humble beginnings and getting to where I am today came down to two key factors: my parents' relentless focus on education, and the physical and mental resilience built through the work experiences of my formative years.

I grew up in a tiny village of about 800 people, twenty miles south of the Danish border—Viking territory, if that tells you anything. My great-grandparents on my mother's side had lost everything in World War II. After fleeing the former eastern territories—now part of modern-day Russia and Poland—they started over with a small shoe repair shop in northern Germany.

My grandmother on my mother's side, clearly not born into wealth, somehow managed to put her two children through university on a single income. She was a 'disgraced' divorcee with only a middle school education and a secretary job at the marine department. While the family remembers her differently, to me she was always the ultimate boss-bitch bootstrapper. Her street credibility was legit and her authority was often relentless. On my father's side, my grandparents lost the family business after the patriarch died because they lacked the right successor. In my family, we are used to starting over and re-building from zero.

My childhood was idyllic in the classic, country living sense. Because there was not much to do except riding bikes and horses, I spent my early years mostly around farmers and horse and cattle-traders. From them, I learned the art of bargaining and deal-making at a very young age.

In Germany, education has always been the determining factor for social advancement, so my parents—both teachers—always placed a high value on academic achievement. A merely average student throughout school, I gave them much reason for disappointment and concern. I was always more of an outdoors, street-smarts kid than a bookworm. And a work horse.

The first time I negotiated my salary was at the age of fourteen. When my parents' allowance wasn't cutting it, I snuck out of the house on weekend nights to work (illegally because I was underage) in the kitchen of our local village pub. From 5 p.m. to sometimes six or seven in the morning, I was washing dishes (by hand and bent over deep kitchen sinks back in those days) for weddings and other events which tended to run long. It was back-breaking work, unimaginable by today's automation standards.

I've also done some of the dirtiest jobs imaginable in the pig and dairy farming industries. Working fourteen-to-sixteen-hour days alongside migrant workers from Poland and Romania was the standard, and I often performed tasks that even they weren't asked to do. Pest control was a trainee favorite. Scraping the frozen carcasses of piglets who hadn't made it out of commercial freezer units for rendering plant pickup was another. Fun times. To 'round out' my profile and fund my second graduate education, I also worked in residential cleaning, public facility maintenance, hospitality, and retail.

These experiences shaped me. They taught me to speak to anyone—with humor, dignity, and respect—whether it's the chairman of the board, the janitor, or a general laborer. They also gave me a deep, empathetic understanding of hard physical work and a high level of resilience.

The fact that it all came together in the end is owed to a lot of starting over, getting back up, and a few lending hands during pivotal moments whenever I thought I had reached the end of the road. To this day, I believe that someone was watching over me back in my early St. Louis days. After 300 rejections and out of sheer desperation, I had applied for an internship in the Communications and PR department of a multinational business services company. As I mentioned at the beginning of the book, it was the only call I ever received for an interview. It was an act of true selfless generosity by an incredible lady named Laura.

Laura could have hired someone far more qualified, and she knew it. Given my language barrier, I was objectively the worst marketing intern they ever had. But I showed up on time every day and did my best, which is the only solid strategy when you're below even the janitor in rank and pay. My first American salary was $20K per year with no benefits or health insurance. I still couldn't afford lunch, but damn it, I was in, and I wasn't mopping the floor or washing dishes. Things were looking up! The fact that she took a chance on me is something I will pay forward for the rest of my life.

Finally, that first opportunity to get my bearings opened other avenues, just as Laura had always assured me. Eventually, I clawed my way into corporate HR. By perfecting the art of financials-based resume writing, I learned to put the oxygen mask on for myself first and pushed open new doors for professional advancement. Later, once I was in, leaders remembered and leveraged my resume writing skills for their own promotions or external job searches.

Knowing that every paycheck I earned was owed to them, I was glad to help. Soon, I began to get passed around, cutting my teeth in different sectors and functions—initially in Finance, Controlling, and Accounting, and later across technology and many other areas. What started as pro-bono work inadvertently became the training ground for ABREO years later.

With a select group of happy clients—many from the executive education communities of Harvard, Wharton, and Stanford—and the support of mentors and advocates, the practice grew, and so did I.

Looking back, everything has come full circle. From building the niche skill set to elevate my own profile and carve out my career, to everything I learned about executive compensation, career transitions, and terminations during my time in corporate HR. The pro-bono resume writing and career coaching journey that allowed me to serve world-class leaders as private clients and establish my practice. Ultimately, all of this led to corporate outplacement partnerships, not only because of our quality but because CHROs know that departing leaders are in good hands with us *as people*.

My own early days American experience makes me relatable for senior executives who often grind through similar experiences in their post-exit search journey. It's something that can't be simply explained—it has to be lived in order to be empathetically understood. Beyond the technicalities and skills required for executive market re-entry preparation, much of what we do is empathy and inspirational work. Every day, we encourage leaders who feel deflated after a difficult termination to keep pushing forward and treat the process as a numbers game.

It doesn't matter if they hate hearing this. It doesn't matter if some tell us, *"Shut up, you haven't been through what I've been through."* I have. Having truly seen it all, I also know the next opportunity will come. For many seasoned executives, fishing for work—often for the first time in their careers—presents an enormous resilience challenge. Finding that next opportunity is not a matter of 'if,' but 'when.' Time is on their side, as long as they're willing to do 'more' in the process, outwork their competitors, leverage their network, and stick with it.

Doing more has always worked out for me. Given where you are today, I know it has paid off for you too so far. You know what you're made of. Chances are you have also cut your teeth on earlier challenges. You too hold attributes like grit, strength, and a steadfast commitment to personal and professional growth within you just like many of our featured protagonists.

In the end, we are not so different in how we build our kingdoms.

CONCLUSION:

The Boss? It's You.

Per ardua ad astra
(Through adversity to the stars)

After supporting top-level executives for over a decade in various capacities, the consistent common denominator has always been that great careers are both earned—and made—self-made, specifically. In today's world, the 'kings' of our time no longer rise through ancestral lineages of royalty, but are, as you saw with our featured leaders, bold DIY bootstrappers.

We often don't pause to reflect on the deeper meaning of 'self-made,' which really means 'to make something happen yourself.' If we break it down, making something happen requires taking action. Taking action requires making a choice. Making a choice requires thought, and thinking about it requires adopting a boss-level mindset and an overall inner attitude of being open to change.

As you prepare for your next chapter as a high-profile leader, I hope the wisdom in *Like A Boss* has inspired you to treat your career more like a business and put things in motion in your outer and inner worlds. Whether you love what you do or see work more as a means to an end, one reality remains unchanged: work is not charity. Money matters. Security matters. The freedom to do whatever you want with your life matters.

Staying prepared for transitions, expanding your learning scope, seeking competitive pay, and protecting your downsides and assets are all essential for securing your future and building generational wealth. Ultimately, the responsibility for this will always rest with you. While it's true that self-advocacy can't be outsourced, wise leaders know their limits. Many top-level executives successfully maximize their career paths and transitions with ABREO's guidance and proactive preparation.

Whether it's translating your achievements into measurable financial outcomes to give your resume a competitive edge and elevate the quality of your hiring conversations, seeking consulting support on negotiating total comp and severance so you get better at not leaving money on the table, or navigating the executive search and legal spaces, it's easier to learn in a community than by mistake. It's also cheaper. If we don't invest in learning, the costs of our mistakes tend to compound unfavorably in the long run. Feel free to reach out to us if you would like our support in the market re-entry space.

If you are a Corporate Legal or Human Resources Executive and feel compelled to learn how we can help you de-risk high-profile exit scenarios, we would love to earn a few minutes of your time. Allow us to become your partner. Let us show you the value you, your company, and the departing executive *should* receive in the market re-entry space. We can help you end difficult exits on a more positive note and lead to successful transitions both for your organization and your departing employee.

On the evening I signed that life-changing first job offer, I drove back into the business district where I had experienced the breakdown I shared in the preface. It was finally my moment to celebrate. Parked on the rooftop of a public parking garage, I had a Chinese lantern with me. Attached to it was a piece of paper with the words: *"Dream big. You got this. Smile."*

Sadly, I later learned that releasing Chinese lanterns wasn't exactly legal in Missouri, so I only did it that one time. But watching its growing flame shine brighter as it ascended into the starry evening sky was a beautiful moment. And I guess also bonus points for not burning down the city.

While unknowingly breaking the law, that lantern moment brought me immense clarity. Even though I didn't know where my light's final destination would be, I understood that I could always bet on myself to lead my own way toward whatever the future had in store for me. I was on my way to building my kingdom.

As I watched my lantern drift toward an unwritten future, all I knew was that I would probably always have to do things a little differently. Most likely, you will lead yourself in a similar way. On your continued journey toward even greater success, you'll likely think more disruptively, break a few rules here and there, self-advocate more, push past some fears, adjust your inner attitude, and build relationships with quality people who will help you evolve. The kind of people who will show up for you in the right way and reciprocate all your heartfelt efforts, both in business and in life.

Given how far you've already come, it's clear that you're poised for even greater growth. There may be some levers you're not yet ready to pull, and you might stumble here and there, having to get back up, practice, and try again. Other areas you might start to build gradually—either now or later. All of this is a natural part of your growth journey and you have every reason to be optimistic about your future.

Just always remember that applying what you learned from *Like A Boss* requires finesse. Out in the real world, you won't plot a,b,c in a predetermined sequence of steps and find all runs smoothly just the way you want it. As an intuitive leader you will understand that the strategies in this book don't create value in and of itself; they don't live and breathe in a vacuum devoid of power and social dynamics.

They require, *and deserve*, to be paired with your emotional intelligence, empathy, intuition, and timing skills. That's why reaching the higher leadership levels is not just science but an art. Hopefully *Like A Boss* provided you some of the lesser-known science areas—and a bit of art too—in how to lead yourself more successfully through life's never-ending ups and downs.

The universe always favors the worthy one—just trust yourself and go. Show up for yourself. Evolve. Level up and bootstrap that next step. Be that slingshot for others and enrich their lives with joy. Leverage your wisdom. Elevate yourself towards the kind of status and gravitas that will leave others in awe about what you are capable of. Light that lantern. Build that kingdom.

I hope you will build the career you want—on your terms—and create a life that excites you every single day. It will set you free.

Grow, rise, shine.
To the stars and forever *Like A Boss*.

Acknowledgements

This book wouldn't have been possible without the incredible boss-level people who walked with me on my personal and professional paths. Thank you to:

My parents and grandparents. I'm so grateful for this life. I love you.

Dr. Bill Allen. For being my dearest friend and mentor. Your patience and wisdom are not something I will ever be able to repay in this lifetime.

Lindsey Sterzik. For your unwavering business support and friendship throughout the years. ABREO would not be where it is today with you.

Stefan Mecha. Ginger Porter. Carol Scott. You are a true force. I'm proud to know you and call you a friend.

Our private and outplacement executive clients. For your courage to be vulnerable and share your successes and teachable moments with us so the tide can rise for all boats.

The many **Board Directors, Chief Human Resources Officers, Chief Legal Officers, and Executive Recruiters** for supporting *Like A Boss*. Thank you for contributing story examples and anonymous quotes and encouraging me to write this book. It is progressive thinkers and leaders like you who quietly drive change from the shadows of major corporations. Without any expectation for public recognition, it is you who help create brighter futures for all of us. You are the unsung heroes of this book.

Thank you for your support, professional opportunities, friendship, encouragement, advocacy, opening your home when I did not have one, guidance, feedback, client referrals, business introductions, speaking engagements, your selfless service to others, plane conversations, travel memories, check-in calls, late-night pizza deliveries, teaching me the art and science of getting fired like a boss, and the inspiration to build an American life that is truly—and finally—free:

Michele Adams. Marcelo Alves. Theresa Bayer. Leslie Beale. Bob Black. Anthony Bond. Emily Burgess. Kelly Carpenter. Melissa Collette. Craig Cook. Britt Cumbie. Royston Da Costa. Pam deVeer. Patty Dignon. Derek Doyle. Andrew Duy. Michael Farrow. Tom Flies. Dan George. Donna Glenn. William Graham. Cord Gumpert. Somer Hackley. Thomas Hanna. Magda and Ralf Himmelreich. Pamela Holz. Kim Holleman. Patty Hoppenstedt. Bill Jones. Gregory L. Jones. Attila Khan. Brandy Kiniry. Debrah Knight. Dr. Susanne Kortendick. Stephanie Lanier. John Lansche. Nanette Levin.

Donata Lingenthal. Susan and John Malanowski. Kristin Martinez. Laura McAllister. Dave McCormick. Michele Molden. Kim Morgan. Chris Murdock. Mark Myers. Diana Needham. Paul Oakley. Anna Pannier. Lee-Ann Perkins. Son Pham. Jon Puncochar. Jenna Quinn. Katie Radel. Prakash Ranjan. Birgit Rieffel. Pedro Rojas. Nichole Sammon. Frau Schwarz. Gina Scott. Sanjeev Sehgal. Sherri Sklar. Victoria Ryan. Heidi Tieslau. Jorge Titinger. Manfred Ubert (decd). Detlef van den Bergh. Prof. Marieta Velikova. Vin Vera. Cindy Weidmann. Donald Wobbe.

You made me a better person in business and in life. May the universe forever bless you with abundance.

About the Author

Elisabeth Constantin, M.A., M.Ed., is a German-American Executive Transition Entrepreneur dedicated to helping leaders maximize their careers, navigate high-profile transitions, and elevate their status and gravitas.

After more than a decade of supporting executive career transitions in corporate HR across the global manufacturing, IT consulting, bioengineering, and raw materials industries in the Americas, Europe, and the Middle East, she founded ABREO Executive Services in 2021.

Initially serving the Ivy League Executive Education communities of Harvard, Wharton, and Stanford, her company has since expanded into a premier corporate outplacement partner specializing in high-profile executive terminations.

ABREO helps leaders competitively position themselves for market re-entry, navigate the executive search landscape, and protect their downside. Her clients include senior leaders from Fortune 500 organizations, including Porsche, Bridgestone, Goldman Sachs, Walmart, Xerox, Microsoft, KFC, HCA, Visa, and Shell.

Prior to launching her executive transition firm, Elisabeth built a career in Marketing, Communications, and B2B Commerce before transitioning into global HR service delivery, total rewards, and expatriate consulting after moving to the United States.

A sought-after speaker on executive and C-suite career ROI, she has been invited to present at Ivy League Clubs across the U.S., the Harvard Business School National Women's Association, and leading corporations and industry organizations, including Dell Technologies, Financial Executives International (FEI), the Association for Corporate Growth (ACG), and EuroFinance (The Economist Group).

Educated in Germany, Elisabeth furthered her executive education at Harvard Business School in Cambridge, MA. She serves on the board of the Center for Global Citizenship at Belmont University and is based in Nashville, Tennessee. In her free time, she enjoys global travel, philanthropy, road cycling, and exploring the great outdoors.

Additional Resources

Atkins, B. (2019). Be Board Ready: The Secrets to Landing a Board Seat and Being a Great Director. New Type.

Greene, R. (2000). The 48 Laws of Power. Penguin Books.

Hackley, S. (2022). Search in Plain Sight: Demystifying Executive Search. New Degree Press.

Mack, O. (2022). Get on Board Earning your Ticket to a Corporate Board Seat. Business Expert Press.

Moyo, D. (2023). How Boards Work And How They Can Work Better in a Chaotic World. Little, Brown.

Tracy, B. (2017). Eat That Frog: 21 Great Ways to Stop Procrastinating and Get More Done in Less Time (3rd ed.). Berrett-Koehler Publishers.

Notes on Sources

Introduction: This Book Will Challenge You!

1. Harter, Jim. 2024. "In New Workplace, U.S. Employee Engagement Stagnates." https://www.gallup.com/workplace/608675/new-workplace-employee-engagement-stagnates.aspx.

Chapter 1: How Your Competitors Think: What You're Up Against

2. Federer, Roger. 2024. "2024 Commencement Address by Roger Federer at Dartmouth." YouTube. www.youtube.com/watch?v=pqWUuYTcG-o.

Chapter 2: How Businesses Think—And What That Means for You

3. Harter, Jim. 2024. "In New Workplace, U.S. Employee Engagement Stagnates." https://www.gallup.com/workplace/608675/new-workplace-employee-engagement-stagnates.aspx.

Chapter 5: Health—Your #1 Priority

4. Our Epidemic of Loneliness and Isolation: The U.S. Surgeon General's Advisory on the Healing

Effects of Social Connection and Community. (n.d.). U.S. Department of Health And Human Services. https://www.hhs.gov/sites/default/files/surgeon-general-social-connection-advisory.pdf

Chapter 13: The Writing On The Wall

5. CNBC. 2020. "JPMorgan CEO Jamie Dimon on being fired: 'It impacted my net worth, not my self worth.'" https://www.cnbc.com/2020/07/21/jpmorgan-ceo-jamie-dimon-on-being-fired.html

6. Peabody, Maryanne, and Larry Stybel. 2001. "The Right Way to Be Fired." Harvard Business Review. https://hbr.org/2001/07/the-right-way-to-be-fired.

7. Weber, Lauren, and Chip Cutter. 2024. "The Most Hated Way of Firing Someone Is More Popular Than Ever. It's the Age of the PIP." Wall Street Journal, November 29, 2024. https://www.wsj.com/business/firing-someone-performance-improvement-plans-more-popular-the-pip-7cac7062.

Chapter 18: Launching Your Board Career Early

8. Corporate Boards USA. (2022, October 24). The role of networking in landing a board position. https://corporateboardsusa.com/2022/10/24/the-role-of-networking-in-landing-a-board-position/

Chapter 28: Change is Always Possible

9. Goldsmith, Marshall, and Mark Reiter. 2007. What Got You Here Won't Get You There: How Successful People Become Even More Successful. N.p.: Hachette Books.

Chapter 31: The Purpose-Learning-Success Triangle

10. Kant, Immanuel. 1992. "An Answer to the Question: What is Enlightenment?" Translated by Ted Humphrey